This book is dedicated to Astrit Panxha!

Bejtullah Destani

ALBANIA:
TO BE OR NOT TO BE?

AUSTIN MACAULEY PUBLISHERS™
LONDON • CAMBRIDGE • NEW YORK • SHARJAH

Copyright © Bejtullah Destani 2023

The right of Bejtullah Destani to be identified as author of this work has been asserted by the author in accordance with sections 77 and 78 of the Copyright, Designs and Patents Act 1988.

All rights reserved. No part of this publication may be reproduced, stored in a retrieval system, or transmitted in any form or by any means, electronic, mechanical, photocopying, recording, or otherwise, without the prior permission of the publishers.

Any person who commits any unauthorised act in relation to this publication may be liable to criminal prosecution and civil claims for damages.

The story, the experiences, and the words are the author's alone.

A CIP catalogue record for this title is available from the British Library.

ISBN 9781398480025 (Paperback)
ISBN 9781398480032 (ePub e-book)

www.austinmacauley.com

First Published 2023
Austin Macauley Publishers Ltd®
1 Canada Square
Canary Wharf
London
E14 5AA

The Contemporary Review & The Centre for Albanian Studies for using photos and maps.

Table of Contents

Introduction for Albania: 'To Be or Not to Be?'   11

The Albanians   23

Albania In Arms   35
   Where There's an Alphabet, There's a Nation   37

Turkey Still the Sick Man of Europe   41
   Diagnosis and Remedies   42
   Young Turkey's Aggressive Nationalism   43
   Young Turkey's Foreign Policy   44
   Young Turkey Becomes Germanophile   45
   Why Young Turkey Cannot Last   47
   Wanton Cruelty of the Young Turks   49
   Loyal Albania Was Driven to Revolt   51
   Russia's Diplomatic Note: The Why and Wherefore   53
   Enter Austria-Hungary   55
   The Conquering Hero Comes Too Late   56
   Autonomy for Albania   58

Roumania and Albania   61
   Albanian Characteristics   63

Albanian Characteristics 67

Benighted Condition of the Albanian People 70

Albania's Strong Man 72

Austria and Italy in Albania 75

The Origin and Aims of Italy's Foreign Policy 76

Italy And Austria In the Adriatic 79

Italy, France, and Great Britain 82

The World Is Tired of The War 86

Petty Tyranny of The Balkan States 87

Impossible Demands of The Allies 89

The Delimitation of Albania 92

Sir Edward Grey's Proposal 94

Bulgaria And the Race for Scutari 96

Sir Edward Grey as Peacemaker 100

Austro-Russian Partial Demobilisation 102

Communiqué and Supplement an Austro-Russian Misunderstanding 104

Alleged Plan to Extirpate the Albanians 105

Austria-Hungary May Intervene in Albania 109

One All-Important Outcome of The Balkan War 111

Germany's Call to Arms and Alms 114

Albania To Be or Not to Be? 118

Albania's Tribulations And Colonel Phillips 124

The Albanian Tangle   **127**

Greece And Turkey Drifting Into War   **170**

Growth of Greco-Turkish Animosity   *172*

A Regenerate Young Turk And A Desperate Problem *175*

Why the Turks Hate and Persecute Their Hellenic Fellow Subjects   *178*

Forcible Transportation of Whole Populations   *180*

Talaat Bey's 'Quos Ego'   *184*

War Loomed in Sight   *187*

The Dawn, or False Dawn, of Peace   *190*

"If I Were King of Arcadia!"   *192*

Will an Albanian Heptarchy Solve the Problem?   *194*

Young Turkey Exclaims: "Barkis Is Willin"   *197*

Introduction for Albania: 'To Be or Not to Be?'

In this unique collection of articles from two of the most prolific, informative and influential journals in Britain, Bejtullah Destani, currently Minister Counsellor for Kosovo in Rome, and founder of the London-based Centre for Albanian Studies, has cleverly brought together an interesting collection of writings by journalist and academic Emile Joseph Dillon related to Albanians and the 'Albanian question' in the period before and during the start of the First World War. Building on the already extensive array of primary source material and contemporary memoirs and commentary he has published, this is another valuable addition from Bejtullah Destani to the printed material relevant to anyone interested in understanding how Albania became independent, problems post-independence, why so many Albanian speakers were excluded from the new Albanian state and the legacy of those decisions for events throughout the twentieth and into the twenty-first centuries.

Dillon's life and career

Despite his many descriptions – journalist, philologist, linguist, academic perhaps the most apt for this collection of works is that which describes Emile Joseph Dillon in one of two works in the National Portrait Gallery in London. When appearing in The New Statesman, Dillon is described in a series of caricatures entitled 'The Men of the Day' as 'The Semi-official Ambassador'. Both epithets are telling – Dillon was considered important, worth drawing, worth writing about and, often took on a diplomatic role. This enabled him to not only witness and describe but to advise, influence, perhaps even shape or steer events that were of paramount importance. As with the 1908–09 Bosnian Annexation Crisis, these contributions were not always welcomed by the British Foreign Office. Whilst his insights and contacts were often useful, his personal connections and relationships, especially with parties not being supported by the British Government at a particular point, could often cause problems.

In seeking to understand Dillon and his perspectives on the Albanian question, it is helpful to consider his wider life and career. It is unclear where his interests in eastern Europe and the Middle East came from but he was certainly an adept linguist and from a relatively early age had generated an interest in Oriental languages and what was they then called 'the Orient'. Born in Dublin in 1854, Dillon (also known by the pseudonym E.B. Lanin), as a second son to an Irish foundry and hardware merchant and English mother was expected to join the priesthood. He soon decided it was not for him. His international training for the priesthood and subsequent studies in Ireland, Wales, France, the United States and various places in eastern and central Europe, especially Germany, where he gained his first doctorate at the University of Leipzig, fostered in him a love of the unusual, a desire for travel, willingness to live in unfamiliar places and a good grounding in a range of foreign languages, especially oriental languages. Dillon officially left the priesthood in 1875, aged 21, but the advantages accrued via his religious training were considerable especially for someone of relatively humble beginnings.

Dillon worked for most his professional life as a linguist and journalist in eastern Europe, particularly in Russia. He appears to have first visited Russia at 23, combining a range of studying, teaching and writing, and gaining two further doctorates. He married a Russian widow, Yelena Maksimovna Bogachova, and had four sons. They divorced in 1913 following a number of alleged affairs with female secretaries, one of whom, Kathleen Mary Ireland, Dillon subsequently married. Despite having a promising academic career, and being renowned as a specialist in Armenian and

Iranian languages, this came to an end when he resigned in protest at the bureaucracy of the Kharkov University where he worked in 1885. It was at this point he turned to journalism, less confined by the constraints of an established organisation and providing a more suitable outlet for his personal opinions and insights.

By the late 1880s, Dillon was well established as a journalist, writing primarily on Russian affairs for the London press, especially The Telegraph, for whom he wrote for nearly 30 years. He also wrote more in-depth pieces in a range of major publications, such as the Fortnightly Review and the Contemporary Review, which both feature here. Dillon's professional highlight, came in 1894–95, when he was able to give a first-hand account of the Armenian Genocide, which horrified the British public and enabled British Prime Minister William Gladstone to indict the Ottoman Government. It was significant too in influencing British foreign policy away from supporting the Ottoman Empire and in favour of the many, primarily Christian, nationalist awakenings in south-eastern Europe. His strong mastery of Armenian as well as other Oriental languages, combined with a strong understanding of their cultures and peoples made him uniquely placed to do so. Dillon's success in Armenia enabled him to develop many close contacts with statesmen, diplomats, and even insurgents, enhancing his reputation as an innovative foreign correspondent. He secured Telegraph agreement for a number of clandestine or covert missions, including most notably reporting on the 1897 revolt in Crete, where he disguised himself as an Orthodox priest living with the Cretan insurgents. Dillon was active in the Balkans during the Bosnian Annexation crisis (1908–09) when his personal relationship with and subsequent public defence of his friend, the Austro-Hungarian foreign minister, Count Alois von Aehrenthal, caused considerable problems for the British Foreign Office in its dealings with Russia. Throughout the 1912–13 Balkan Wars and the start of the 1914–18 First World War, he remained a prolific writer on Balkan topics, although usually from a distance and rarely as a direct observer on the scene. Only one article included by Destani seems to have been written whilst in Albania. Nevertheless, Dillon's earlier exploits prompted William T. Stead, himself once described as 'the most famous journalist in the British Empire' to describe Dillon as 'Britain's premier foreign correspondent'.[1]

By 1917, and despite accurately predicting the fall of the Russian Empire, Dillon seems to have outlived his usefulness to the *Telegraph* and his contributions in other journals became less frequent. He subsequently moved to Mexico and ultimately to Spain. He continued to comment on Russia, the Soviet Union and eastern Europe more generally, including during the Paris Peace Conferences. He was very critical of the Conferences as a way to securing peace, but was not able to have the influence he had in the quarter century before the First World War. Following his death, E. Clerihew Bentley recorded that Dillon was remembered as 'a man of mystery...whose business in life it was to know and understand foreign affairs in a way peculiar to himself'.[2]

---

[1] For more detailed information on the life and career of Dillon please see the excellent citation by Joseph O. Baylen at https://doi.org/10.1093/ref:odnb/32828 (2004, updated 2008), as well as information about him at the National Portrait Gallery, London.

[2] E. C. Bentley, *Those days* (1940), p. 318.

Dillon's views on the Albanian question

The collection or articles covers 1903–15, but with a particular focus on 1911, 1913 and 1914. By this point in his career, Dillon has often been criticised for being increasingly opinionated and divisive, but in this selection, he is generally moderate, commenting on events and accurately foretelling future problems. Admittedly, he may no longer have had the same value of being able to disguise himself and get into situations other journalists could not or would not. Nevertheless, he covers a broad historical and geographical sweep of particular events and episodes relevant to the emergence of an independent Albania and the problems of that state in practice. He is particularly insightful in showing the geopolitical interests of the great powers and the inter-relatedness of the Albanian question to wider European geo-politics.

Dillon had a keen eye for the 'other' or more precisely 'the others' as there were multiple and they were often inter-mingled and inter changing. Whilst not unique in his observations or the only Western commentator, M Edith Durham and Aubrey Herbert being perhaps the best-known examples, Dillon's observations do seem important. The breath of his travels, the variety or his contacts and at all levels, and the array of his languages – he would claim to speak 26 languages, be fluent in 10 – surpass any of the other contemporaries by far to my knowledge, although his understanding of Albanian is unclear and in most of these works, he seems to be commenting from outside Albania. Perhaps most interestingly, unlike Durham, Herbert and other contemporary British or Irish commentators, Dillon does not appear to have been an 'Albanophile'. Whilst Dillon applauds the Albanians as amongst 'the most chivalrous and also most docile' in Europe, he also likens them 'to sharp, rough stones' and on occasion is heavily critical: 'the depth of ignorance in which the bulk of Albanians plunged can hardly be fathomed'. Similarly, with the exception of the Turks, he is generally fairly moderate in his assertions and comments on all the other protagonists, enabling a more holistic, even considered perspective.

Destani's collection starts in 1903 with 'The Albanians' (*Contemporary Review*), which is a useful overview from Dillon's perspective of the history, culture, customs and geography of 'Albania' and 'Albanians', and the complexities and competing interests' other nationalities and states. He makes strong parallels with other minority ethnic groups in the Ottoman Empire, especially the Kurds and Armenians. The next series of chapters show the important role of the Young Turk revolution and centralisation programme in the Albanian question. He talks of a series of more practical problems that made Albanians unsupportive of the Young Turk regime and ultimately becoming the critical factors in awakening Albanian nationalism. Dillon gives a much less positive, often critical, perspective than other commentators, on the Albanians at the time, including on central figures in the national movement (*Albanian Characteristics*). Across several entries, Dillon comments on oft sighted but generally misunderstood aspects of Albanian culture and identity related to vendetta and perceptions of monetary payments (or bribes). He helps to elucidate why the great powers may have had such difficulty in taming or influencing potential

Albanian protégés. He is most passionate and supportive of the Albanians when he returns to concerns about the potential massacre of Albanians in the Second Balkan War ('The World is Tired of the War', *Contemporary Review* 1913).

The book centres around a number of articles in the middle, two of which the wider book is named after 'Albania to be of not to be?' (*Contemporary Review*, 1914) and 'The Albanian Tangle' (*Fortnightly Review*, 1914). Dillon is interestingly silent on the Albanian declaration of independence in November 1912 or the First Balkan War more widely, focusing heavily on the relations between the great powers and the establishment of the new state. In these articles, he demonstrates the difficulties of setting up a new, small and independent state and in delimiting its boundaries, especially when the neighbouring states and great powers are not only not committed to the task, but in many cases actively undermining it, as with the Greeks in southern Albania or northern Epirus. Dillon's assertions, which reflect many of my own views, are that it was wider geo-political interests and *realpolitik* that were responsible for the great powers establishing Albania. He wrote that creating Albania was the 'direct and necessary outcome of the sudden shifting of the equilibrium, in South-Eastern Europe.' Across various chapters, Dillon explores the interests and roles of all the great powers, especially Italy and Austria in determining to create Albania and delimit its boundaries. Despite criticisms elsewhere of his apparent bias towards Austria-Hungary, especially his friend Count Aehrenthal, and similarly the Greek political figure and five-time Prime Minister, Eleutherius Venizelos, in these works he is generally moderate, clearly articulating the various competing issues and geopolitical considerations at play.

Throughout the articles, Dillon shows the difficulties which the new Albanian state had for the powers considered the solution 'transitional' and the 'struggle for national life will begin as soon as the peace has been established' ('The World is Tired of War', *Contemporary Review* 1913). As the last entry, in the *Contemporary Review* (1915), most clearly demonstrates even Austria, previously the most earnest support of Albanian nationalism and independence undertook a *volte face* during the First World War, following the Italian occupation in Vlorë and entry into the war on the other side, in an attempt to secure Greek support for the central powers. This was the precariousness on which an independent Albanian state was created. Without consistent and underlying support, the fate of the state and its people would remain in doubt.

The Albanian question or 'to be or not to be'

It may be helpful for some readers to know a little more about the Albanian 'question' or 'tangle'. The Albanian question for the great powers of Europe, and it was in my view primarily a great power problem not a 'national' question, was what to do with the non-Turkish, non-Arab, mainly Muslim, but also Catholic and Orthodox Christian 'Albanian' speaking people in the western Balkans. Whilst this territory was overwhelming Albanian-speaking these 'Albanians' spoke other languages, were divided by religion and were interlaced with other populations, especially Greeks, Serbs and Vlachs (Romanian speakers). Combined with the strong strategic advantages of 'Albanian territory' on the eastern Adriatic, this produced strong competing ambitions for this territory from the various Slav groups (Serbs, Montenegrins and today

North Macedonians, although not called that then) and the Greeks. These ambitions resulted from the collapse of the Ottoman Empire, the so-called 'sick man of Europe' on the one hand and the rise and resurgence of ethnic nationalism across the many Balkan peoples on the other. Perhaps most important, were the related interests of the European great power sponsors of these small states and new and re-emerging nationalities and nationalisms. Austria-Hungary particularly was not prepared to allow Serbia or Italy to gain a foothold on the eastern Adriatic, effectively cutting off Austria-Hungary from the Mediterranean.

The Albanians proclaimed independence at Vlorë (Valona) on 28 November 1912, as the primary means to avoid consolidation into Serbia, Montenegro, Bulgaria or Greece following the collapse of Turkey-in-Europe in the First Balkan War (1912). Independence was confirmed by the European great powers in the 1912–13 London conferences. A new monarch, a German prince Wilhelm of Wied was inaugurated in March 1914, following the tradition of inserting German princes into new Balkan states. Wied was supported by an International Commission of Control, consisting of representatives of the six European great powers. Two boundary commissions, one in the south and one in the north, were to delimit the boundaries on the ground, save for those towns already agreed by the great powers in concert, including Shkodër (Scutari), Djakova and Korçë (Koritza).

This was not the end of the matter and there continued a long struggle as independence was 'lost' during the First World War. Wilhelm fled as early as September 1914, returning to Germany. Even before this there had been major uprisings, especially in 'northern Epirus', amongst the ethnic Greeks incorporated into the new state. During the First World War, the Albanians returned to rival fractions and fought amongst themselves as much as with the Allies and the central powers. This was in spite of the basis on which Britain supposedly entered the war to protect the independence and sovereignty of another small sovereign and multi-lingual state agreed over 80 years earlier by the great power concert – Belgium. Albanian independence was not settled at the Paris Peace Conferences after the First World War and only finally reconfirmed by the League of Nations on 17 December 1921. It proved to be a continual struggle. The fate of the Albanian people was invariably linked to the great power system, the rivalry between the European great powers and the appetites of the new primarily Christian Balkan states that surrounded the Albanian speakers, all of whom had a greater power sponsor or protector for at least part of this period.

Whilst, the Albanians were ultimately successful in securing an independent state, this was without significant numbers of Albanian speakers in Chameria in Northern Greece, in Macedonia (now Northern Macedonia) and especially in Kosovo. The boundaries of the new state in many cases cut rural populations off from their market towns. Unlike the new Christian-dominated national states, what made Albanians unique was their language (codified and an alphabet agreed only as recently as 1908 but nonetheless recognised as a distinct Indo-European language). Their rivals tried to divide them on the basis of religion and the national principle was further complicated by the fact that most Albanian speakers were bi or multi-lingual, speaking a combination of Greek, Serb, other Slavic dialects, Vlach, Turkish, plus often Italian, German or French, especially for trade. This was despite it being agreed that self-determination on the linguistic principle was paramount, as most famously proclaimed in Woodrow Wilson's 14 points in 1917, but agreed as sacrosanct for the Albanian question as early as the 1912–13 London conferences.

It is easy to talk that 'lessons should have been learned' in the western Balkans. Many of the issues Dillon observed and commented on in the Balkan wars at the start of the twentieth century, mirrored those that persisted in the Balkans wars at the end of the century and at other places across the world, especially where foreign powers have attempted to install a new state or regime. But as Dillon clearly demonstrates throughout the peoples are intertwined and intermingled and there were such significant issues at stake and people's views and positions were constantly changing. Here the book's title – 'the Albanian Tangle' – is particularly apt.

—Nicola Guy

The Contemporary Review, January–June 1903

The Albanians

Even unbiassed Europeans whose first desire is to see war averted at almost any price are sceptical as to the upshot of the 'reforms'. And the more closely they have studied contemporary history, the greater are their misgivings, for the present proceedings seem to them but a superfluous rehearsal of an old show which no longer conjures up even a passing illusion in the minds of the onlookers. Islam, they say, has not modified its character any more than the leopard has changed his spots, and in Turkey, Islam is the faith of conquerors, Christianity the creed of slaves. Between the two, there can be no equality. How then can there be justice or equity? In truth, so long as the administrators are Mohammedans, the Christians will be victims of injustice and worse, and both sides know it. The late poet's secretary – Hilmi Pasha – now Inspector General, is, we are told, an honourable man. So was my friend, Shakir Pasha, who some years ago was appointed Inspector General, with the noble task of introducing reforms into Armenia. And what happened there is a matter of common knowledge and of local regret. Shakir Pasha remained the honourable man he had been, but the Armenians, whose lot he had come to better, were sent to the next world in thousands, and the word 'reform' was thenceforward blotted out of the vocabulary of the people of those parts. Will anything better come of Hilmi's attempt to twist ropes of sand?

The Kurds slaughtered the Armenians; it was they, therefore, and not the Turks who hindered the reforms. Such, at least, is the official version of the episode. In the present case, it is the Albanians who will thwart the well-meant experiments of the sultan, and if they compass this, it is because too large a measure of reforms was insisted upon by the powers. Such is said to be the official forecast. It is a simple sum in political proportion: as the Kurds are to the Armenians, so are the Albanians to the Macedonians, the Porte being wholly eliminated. And this, in official circles in Russia and Austria-Hungary, is regarded as the most formidable danger of all. To the foreigner who is not familiar with the peoples of the Balkan Peninsula, some explanation may be needed. Why, for instance, should the Albanians meddle in other people's affairs? In Kurdistan, Kurds and Armenians lived side by side, and the lot of the one element could not well be modified without that of the other being also influenced for good or evil. But how can reforms in Macedonia affect the Moslems of Albania, whose land is to the west, so directly as to rouse them to resistance? The answer is simple. For the past ten years or more, the Albanians have been slowly extending their territory and without serious opposition. The Macedonian Christians who occupied their own land were either killed off or driven away in large numbers from the Vilayets or provinces of Kossovo, Monastir, Salonika: many of the emigrants seeking refuge in Bulgaria, where, as I pointed out, they constitute, roughly speaking, thirty percent of the civil and military officials of the principality, others settling in Servia. The Albanians have duly taken their places, and so it comes that there is a large sprinkling of these chivalrous brigands in the pashaliks of Uskub, Mitrovitsa, Prizrend, Prishtina and other places – which are all in Macedonia – such a large sprinkling indeed that they constitute the majority of the population. And in the places where they are in the minority, they are nonetheless the predominant element, seeing that they carry weapons openly and know how to use them, while the Christian Serb, Bulgarian and Greek is by law unarmed. This, it must be honestly admitted, is a real difficulty with which the best-willed sultan would find it hard to cope, for the Albanians supply the bravest troops in the Turkish Army and are among the most trusted defenders of the sultan. The dilemma then is this: if the Shadow of Allah allows them to play for their own hand, the reforms and reformed will soon find a sudden and common end. And if he dares to check their opposition, the chances are enormous that they will rise up in arms against the Turks, and an Albanian rebellion would be a much more formidable affair than the most thoroughly organised insurrection in Macedonia.

There is perhaps no more ancient or interesting race in Southern Europe than that of which the 1,100,000[3] Albanians of Albania are the last representatives. Related to the primitive Pelasgian population, which strayed away from the Aryan stock in prehistoric times, they have clung tenaciously ever since to their clannish customs, which helped them to shake off almost every foreign yoke but hindered them from

---

[3] Albanian has, in all, about 1,600,000 inhabitants, of whom 500,000 are Slavs, Greeks, Vlachs, Gypsies, and Jews.

coalescing in one to form a great and powerful political state. With amazing strength, they have withstood all efforts made by the Greeks, Romans, Slavs and Turks to assimilate them. Thus, ethnographical islands of them, like oil-drops in water, have been scattered over Greece[4], and the Appenine Peninsula[5], and although for four and even six centuries they have been thus surrounded by Greeks and Italians, they still speak the language and observe the customs bequeathed to them by their forbears. Geographical position, dialects and characteristic traits divide this people into two sections or tribes, the Ghegs and the Tosks, of whom the former are brave to rashness, faithful to the point of self-sacrifice, and simple in tastes and manners; the latter are more sociable, less warlike, just as devoted to their respective tribes, and almost equally sober, while both are ruinously hospitable and passionately fond of fighting and plundering. In their love of bloodshed and horror of humdrum and laborious lives, they resemble the Kurds and feel like them that they have a better right to exist and thrive than the inferior races who are on earth merely for their sakes. Yet oddly enough, each tribe hates the other with religious rancour, although it is only fair to say that the line of cleavage does not always run parallel with religious tenets. There are, indeed, Roman Catholic, Orthodox and Mohammedan tribes, whose fanaticism seems at times to be greater than that of peoples whose conversion to those creeds is of much older date. Thus, about three-fifths of the people profess to make some rude attempts at practising

---

[4] There are about 200,000 Albanians, chiefly in Attica and Megaris, who still speak their own tongue.
[5] They number about 100,000 and are found principally in Calabria, Terra d'Otranto, and Sicily.

the religion of Mohammed, but many among them were Christians down to the sixteenth or seventeenth centuries, and like the Kurds of Asia Minor still cherish many a Christian belief and follow many a Roman Catholic precept. Indeed, there is said to be quite a considerable number of persons who in secret are still Christians in every respect while openly professing the teachings of Islam. Then again, there are numerous Roman Catholics among them – the Mirdites[6], for instance – who, occupying inaccessible fortresses, never allow a Mussulman to abide in their territory, on any pretext. And yet on the whole, religious cares sit lightly upon the broad shoulders of the Albanians, who are linked together by a primitive organisation based upon clans and families, the duties towards which generally take precedence over every other consideration, human and divine. Thus, half the members of a tribe may be Christians and the other half Moslems, while all the members are united as one man in the defence of their tribal customs. Again, the Christian clergy sometimes wield enormous influence over the laymen of their clans, even when many of the latter profess and practise the religion of Mohammed. On the other hand, Roman Catholic and Orthodox priests – who in Albania wear long moustachios – have no scruples about shouldering a rifle any more than they have to wave a cross, and Christian laymen who frequent the church think nothing of imitating their polygamist brethren.

Neither Mohammedans nor Christians are chary of bloodshedding. 'Death is better than fear' is one of their most favourite proverbs. One of the reasons is the circumstance that

---

[6] There are between 25,000 and 28,000 strong.

education can hardly be said to exist. 'He who has often been avenged is wiser than he who has been taught much' is another of their characteristic sayings, which throws light on their views on these matters. There is a solitary Albanian school for girls at Kortcha, carried on by Americans. Three lay schools are supported by Italy, who has made several praiseworthy attempts to educate and unite the people and to inspire them with a national idea instead of the merely tribal interests, which have so long kept them in feud with each other. But unfortunately, the Italian Government has not had the courage of its opinions nor the energy called for by its interests. Thus, it allowed excellent schools in Prevesa, Valona and Durazzo to be suppressed in 1891, and it has not even attempted to add a school of crafts and trades to the excellent establishment which is still doing such good work in Scutari, nor has it given any practical encouragement to the project of opening a railway from Durazzo and Valona to Monastir. Austrian Jesuits are gradually supplanting Italian Franciscans; Austrian post-offices are at work in Yanina and San Giovanni di Medua; an Austrian hospital treats the sick poor gratuitously in Scutari; Austrian religious congregations push the interests of their government in Valona, Durazzo, Prizrend and Scutari, and the Society of Navigation, which has practically monopolised the coasting trade, is also Austrian.

But foreign influence in Albania is restricted to the few towns. The wave of civilisation has not even sprinkled with its foam the life of the people in the interior, whose besetting passion is a love of arms and booty, as in olden times. Impatient of every yoke, they have maintained virtual independence against every foreign power, from the Greeks to the Turks, and today are as free as the Hungarians or the Canadians and as lawless as the Kabyles. "Fire, water and Governments," says their proverb, "know no mercy." So, they have freed themselves from the government of outsiders and to a great extent of their own people as well. The Tosks are supposed to pay but little taxes and do not always fulfil this obligation, while the Ghegs pay none at all but merely agree to furnish a contingent to the Ottoman Army in wartime, having first entered it in the seventh century, ever since when they have formed the nucleus of the sultan's best fighting troops. The landowners dwell in fortified houses, their retainers are armed to the teeth, and the wherewithal to live is furnished by the Christians – Bulgarians, Serbs, or Greeks – who, wise in their generation, lay in corn, fruits or money which their enemies enjoy. The Malesia tribe of Dibra, for example, is supported almost exclusively by the proceeds of organised depredations on the Slavs who try to live and work in their neighbourhood. The Turkish Government possesses neither the power nor the will to meddle with the tribal customs of which this is at once the most popular and most profitable. Its attitude is based on the Albanian proverb which tersely says, "He who will not support a cat must feed mice."

Vendetta and hospitality are the two tribal customs, the strict observance of which make the most profound impression on the foreigner. Not only do sanguinary feuds rage for generations between two tribes but also between two families of the same tribe, and hundreds of persons are sacrificed at sight to propitiate the blood-thirsty shades of parents or forbears. It has been calculated that about twenty-five percent of the entire population die violent deaths. But the prospect has no terror for the Albanian whose proverb expresses his feelings on the subject: "Dying is a plague, but it is half a plague to live." At times, large tracts of land are given over to these sanguinary encounters, and oddly enough, while any man passing there may be shot down by his enemy or the enemy of his tribe, a woman is allowed to go her way unmolested. Hospitality, too, is carried to extraordinary lengths, and the murderer of a man can trust his victim's family to spare his life once he has gained the shelter of their home. To the average Albanian, the tribe is the state. The standard-bearer (bairaktar) is its president in peace, its chieftain in war. All important questions are decided by a meeting of elders appointed by lot, but such grave issues as the declaration of war, the conclusion of peace, or the change of any customs which constitute the unwritten law of the people are adjudged upon by a popular body, to which every house deputes a representative with a right to vote. A warlike and really capable people like the Albanians would have long since won absolute independence and founded a powerful state in the Balkans, had it not been for the utter absence of any national strivings or ideals. During all the centuries of their chequered existence, they have never advanced beyond the tribal stage, not even when the Albanian League was founded at Turkey's instigation (1878) in order to work for the restitution of Gusinye and Plava to Albania. Efforts have indeed been made of late to weld all the tribes together and nerve them to strike a blow for independence, but so long as the movement has its headquarters in Belgium, Rumania, or anywhere outside the country, and is deprived of the help which education alone can confer, it has no chance of success.

Italy, indeed, has merited well of Albania and its people, having more than once endeavoured to induce the Porte to relax the law which proscribes Albanian schools with instruction in the native tongue, but in vain. Indeed, of all the foreign powers which have heretofore displayed a political interest in the people and country, Italy's aims, if not any more disinterested than those of her rivals, have been immeasurably more advantageous to the Albanians themselves. Autonomy is the ideal for which the bulk of Italian statesmen are striving, for they are by no means desirous of seeing the land cut up and divided among a number of states, and their reasons must and will be duly listened to. Whatever may be said of Italy's historic rights to the Albanian seaboard – and from this point of view her case seems strong enough – it is quite certain that so long as she remains a first-class power, she cannot allow either Austria to annex or protect the country or Montenegro to assimilate it. For Italians, the road to the Black Sea leads over Albania, along the old Via Egnatia; Albania commands the entrance to the Adriatic which has been picturesquely described as one of the lungs through which Italy breathes and lives. There are several gulfs and ports on its coast which in the hands of a military power would enable it to checkmate Italy forever; it is certain in time to possess, as in the old Roman days, one of the chief commercial routes of Europe, joining the peoples of the western side of the Mediterranean with those of the Balkan States. Now a great power which should firmly establish itself in Albania would be mistress of the Adriatic, and Italy might then furl her standards and humbly apply for the protectorate of that or some other powerful state[7].

---

[7] The reader who is interested in the international aspect of this question may read with advantage the admirable work, *L'Albania*

But the interest which is felt just now in Albania springs less from the role which it is destined to play in international policy than from the attitude its impulsive people are likely to take up on the subject of the reforms in the Macedonian provinces, which are gradually becoming Albanised. That fierce, lawless tribes like those which now inhabit the vilayets of Kossovo and Monastir, and have always successfully shaken off the Turkish yoke, should quietly let themselves be tamed by a few gendarmes, should uncomplainingly give up customs more sacred to them than the dictates of religion to Christians, should work hard for their livelihood instead of robbing mere Giaours, and should treat the latter as equals and worthy of respect, is a set of propositions which no man can seriously entertain who has realised their meaning. The thing is simply inconceivable; it would in truth be easier far to force Englishmen to let themselves be governed by the Baboos of Bengal than to get the Albanians to give up the customs of their ancestors and their wild love of freedom for the sake of a race which loathing they cannot even hate. If the Russian or Austrian Ambassador in Constantinople imagines that this task will be accomplished by the Porte, he must be in possession of data as yet unknown to anyone else. Those who have most carefully studied the elements of the problem are the first to recognise that the Albanian difficulty is far more serious than any outbreak among the Macedonians can be, however successful it may seem at the outset.

---

by Arturo Galanti (Roma, 1901), and the pamphlets, *I Rapporti tra l'Italia e l'Albania* (Firenze, 1901); In *Giro sui Confini d'Italia* (Roma, 1899); or the interesting articles which Francesco Guicciardini published under the title: *Impressioni d'Albania* in the *Nuova Antologia*, Vol. XCIII., Serle iv., and Vol. XCIV., Serie iv., June, July, 1901.

Foretokens of the coming storm have been noted by the political meteorologists of the Balkans. Thus, five Albanian tribes recently sent their delegates to Djakova to discuss their future line of action. Numerous other assemblies are also being called together to deliberate openly in Ipek, Djakova, and throughout the vilayet of Uskub and secretly elsewhere. The assembly held near Djakova regards the introduction of reforms into certain provinces and not into others as an attempt to split up Albania which they cannot brook, but they have not yet put forward that objection in words. They have, however, protested against reformed law courts, against Turkish high schools, and against the employment of Christians in the gendarmes and police. Hilmi Pasha, who was informed of the meeting, despatched Muretsa Pasha and Shaban Pasha to Djakova for the purpose of inducing the notables to forego their opposition, but these dignitaries might as well have whistled songs to a milestone. Then Hafiz, the Vali of Uskub, invited the leader of the malcontents to pay a visit to Uskub and talk the matter quietly with him, but to this request, they did not deign even to reply. A telegram was then forwarded to Yildiz Kiosk, informing the sultan that 20,000 Albanians of the districts in question were at His Majesty's orders, but that they were resolved to resist the introduction of any reforms which might seem detrimental to their interests. In addition to all this, it should be borne in mind that the Grand Vizier, Ferid Pasha, is himself an Albanian.

The Russian Press – possibly Russian diplomacy as well – is growing alive to this rock ahead. The Novoye Vremya writes: "On the Balkan horizon looms a new danger, which threatens to upset all the peaceful plans of Europe. This danger lies in the Albanians[8]." Albanian gendarmes recently arrested, bound, and maltreated some Russian monks in Old Servia, who had come from Mount Athos to defend by their presence the ancient Detchan Monastery which had been practically restored with money granted by the tsar. In Old Servia, especially the Albanians hate the Slavs, for among their number are many Mahommedan landowners who have been driven from Servia. That these fierce tribes will meekly sacrifice their secular rights for these same Slavs is out of the question, and this fact is known in Vienna as well as in St Petersburg. It explains, too, why the sultan so quickly accepted the reforms and why he is now hurrying on his preparations for war. The truth is that no set of acceptable reforms can be realised in Macedonia by means of diplomatic pressure only. Moreover, the sultan knows that the unanimity of the powers would not stand the test of an effort to force him to fulfil his promise. The utmost one can hope, and only optimists venture to allow themselves the luxury, is that a short breathing time may be gained and the catastrophe meanwhile put off. What may be relied upon as certain is that the very modest reforms which the Christian Powers have made a show of offering to their protégés are on paper and will remain there until the three provinces known as Macedonia have passed out of the hands of the Shadow of Allah.

E. J. Dillon

---

[8] *Novoye Vremya*, February 8, 1903.

The Contemporary Review, January–June 1910

Albania In Arms

Life's little ironies are unusually common and caustic in the sphere of international politics, owing, among other causes, to the double sets of weights and measures that are openly used there. Quod licet Jovi non licet bovi is one of the practical maxims that give rise to misunderstandings and sometimes let in the tide of desolating war. A cynic would find inexhaustible food for his peculiar meditations behind the scenes of the political theatre: gazing upon Poles treading down Russians in Galicia and enduring persecution at the hands of Russians in the Warsaw of Muravieff; Finns wrestling for their home rule with the Russian giant, yet persecuting the helpless Jew and forbidding him to enter their principality; Persians who, having fought by proxy and won by proxy their freedom from absolutism, now putting summarily and ferociously to death men whose sole offence is their fidelity to the deposed Shah; Young Turks who, after having preached tolerance and freedom of opinion for a generation in Paris, Geneva and London, then practised Hamidism with three-legged gallows in Constantinople, hanging men who had differed from them in opinion but were quite willing to change their views and be sociable. A curious version oriental of popular parliamentary government! And now we have the rising in Albania as one of the consequences of this 'constitutional *regime*'.

In truth, Young Turkism is a peculiar creed of politics. It reserves its liberal principles for its friends and the three-legged gallows and other practical appliances for its enemies, a class that includes all who are not its active allies. With the Albanians, the quarrel of Young Turkey was avoidable, needless, wanton. "The Albanians," an ambassador to the Porte recently assured a pressman, "are savages, who cannot settle down in a well-ordered state and have to be castigated- paternally, of course." Now that is a euphemism that wanders into the region of pure fiction. The Albanians are a high-spirited, chivalrous, life-contemning race. True, they think nothing about snuffing out human life or keeping up a blood feud until every member of the hostile family lies under the sod. But they are not savages. On the contrary. Moreover, they belong to a trace whose intellectual equipment is very much superior to that of the Turk-nay, to that of the Italians, the French and Germans. This is not a paradox nor a piece of flattery, it is a scientific fact, or what should pass for one, seeing that it is stamped with the authority of the late Prof. Virchow, who gave it as his opinion that the Albanian skull showed a higher degree of intellectual power than that of any other European race. Fighting has always been their native element and they grace it with a kind of chivalry that is worthy of the days of Saladin. No foreign government has ever yet subdued the Albanian highlands – neither Venetian nor Turk.

Where There's an Alphabet, There's a Nation

About thirty years ago, there were two Albanian brothers – Fracheri by name – who headed a literary movement, of which the aim was the cultivation of the national language of the country. Educated in Europe, these men chose the Latin alphabet, because it was simpler and much apt to express the sounds of Albanian than, Turkish or Greek, and they thus made it possible for their fellow countrymen to have a written language of their own. This literary national endeavour was favoured later on by the Young Turkish party, which remained a staunch friend of the Albanians until it suddenly came into power. And then it became a paternal castigator.

The Young Turkish revolution of 1908 clove the two movements, and one of the first acts of the new régime was to establish order among Albanians of the north. The officer sent to chastise these unruly tribes was Djavid Pasha, a man of iron hand and stony heart, whose ideal of order resembled the ideal of peace outlined by Tacitus in three or four words. Castles, villages, stone towers, blockhouses were simply wiped out of existence by Djavid's mountain guns, which were silenced at last by the wintry mountain blasts. But the persistent Turkish commander organised two further campaigns against the Albanians and occupied Ipek, Djakova, and other places, including the 'impregnable fastnesses' of the Malissors. Then he informed the central government in Constantinople that he had accomplished the mission confided to him and restored order and law. That was in June last year. In July, the trouble broke out afresh, and even Young Turkish Albanians gave voice to their indignation at the ferocity of Djavid. The most popular cry just then was: "First give us schools and afterwards gather the taxes."

The meaning of that phrase was this: the Albanians had been forbidden by the strictly constitutional Anglo-parliamentarian Government of regenerate Turkey to use the Latin alphabet for their language. A constitutional, tolerant government forbidding an alphabet is a sight not to be forgotten in the twentieth century. But the sting of that curious law lay in the circumstance that the Albanians had, out of private funds of their own, provided schools in which their language and literature were taught and the Latin alphabet used. In these schools, with which the Ottoman Government had nothing to do, the Arabic alphabet was now introduced by force. And it was against the innovation that the outcry was raised. In this connection, too, the saying quoted in the headline received currency: "Where there's an alphabet there's a nation." That was one of the elements of the quarrel. It was instrumental in leading to the murder of the commander of Ipek, Rushdi Bey, by an Albanian. And then the smouldering fires of discontent were fanned to flame, and the real troubles began.

In the rapidity with which the Ottoman Government has conjured up an army, which is powerful enough to wage a regular campaign even against a foreign foe, one can discern the grim pleasure which the energetic war minister feels at the opportunity thus afforded him of showing to Europe what manner of military feats Turkey, at a pinch, is capable of achieving. One seems to hear Mahmoud Shefket Pasha say to Europe: "You have forbidden us to punish Greece. You have barred our way to Crete. But remember, we have drawn the line there. We are glad to live in peace with our neighbours.

But if any of our neighbours should be unwilling to live in peace with us, let them see that we also know how to carry on war. Look!"

Under Abdul Hamid, an insurrection in Albania would have sent a thrill of apprehension through Europe. First, because of the difficulties of the campaign. On the map, Albania has a rugged and forbidding aspect. It is a land wrinkled with a multitude of little mountain ranges, a diminutive Switzerland, a mountainous country abounding in passes easy to hold and hard to capture; a national fortress manned with warriors who are inseparable from their rifles, which they regard as the outward and visible sign of the freeborn man. And to tame these children of rugged nature is a knotty problem. As we saw, Djavid Pasha, who spared neither fire nor shells nor human lives, flattered himself two years ago that he had 'tranquillised the country', only to find it as disturbed as ever a few weeks later. And, under the Hamidian régime, even such military successes as Djavid obtained were beyond the reach of the Ottoman Army.

The second ground for trepidation which Europe would have had in the days before the revolution would have arisen from the fateful question which each one of a whole group of powers would have put itself: "Which of us is going to annex Albania now, and what sort of a sop will be thrown to the remainder?" For Albania has long been part of the legacy to be left by the 'dying man' of Turkey, and each of the heirs longed for it wistfully. Several times it has been the object of negotiations between the powers, as for example, in 1897, between Count Goluchowski on the part of Austria, and Visconti-Venosta as the representative of Italy, each side undertaking to abstain from interference in Albania without first consulting with the other. And now Albania has been eliminated from the list of 'spheres'. It is neither a sphere of influence, nor a sphere of interest. It is an integral part of the Ottoman Empire: that and nothing more. And that change is being accentuated now by the heavy guns of the government. The upshot of the struggle is a foregone conclusion. Time and money will be sacrificed, but Albania will assuredly be punished and tamed. Over the accounts of the campaign published by enterprising newspapers, one might aptly write: "A Warning to All Whom it May Concern."

E. J. Dillon

The Contemporary Review, July 1911

Turkey Still the Sick Man of Europe

Turkey is still the witches' cauldron in which Protean dangers to the world's peace continue to be brewed. The revolution has changed only names; the vis inertice has perpetuated the things they connoted. Today, political writers aim their arrows of barbed criticism at the young instead of the old Turk's Head. But the target is still the Turk's Head, as it used to be when Abdul Hamid was vigorous and powerful. Every statesman in Europe – or at any rate on the continent of Europe – is carefully regulating his policy with an eye to what may happen in the 'Ottoman' Empire tomorrow, in six months, or in a year's time. That something startling and deep-reaching, something affecting the destinies of Europe will take place someday unexpectedly is a foregone conclusion. Everything points that way. No government really believes that the Young Turkish régime is going to last, and few imagine that when it goes, the 'Ottoman' Empire will survive it for long. It is fair to add, however, that some foreign secretaries honestly think that Young Turkey possesses vital force enough to carry it over all its difficulties, if only this or that efficacious measure were adopted, this or that salutary direction were determined upon. But unless these precautions be taken, the Sick Man – for Turkey is still the Sick Man who has temporarily developed unwonted strength – is bound to give up the ghost very soon.

Diagnosis and Remedies

The remedies prescribed differ according to the diagnosis, and opinions on both points are numerous. According to some political experts, secrecy is the poison that is undermining the constitution of Young Turkey. A systematic endeavour to govern an empire composed of many conflicting races, tongues and religions, by hole-and-corner edicts coming from obscure individuals who lack training and shirk responsibility, is bound to lead to disaster. Let these real masters of Young Turkey raise their vizors, come into the open, accept responsibility and brook criticism, and the malady will forthwith disappear. Then you will see green buds swell and shoot up from the old dry stick as in the days of sinful Tannhäuser. Constitutional Government, as in England, is the one infallible cure for all nations that, like Turkey, are jaded with suffering and demoralised by despotism. Introduce the Parliamentary system, play the game fairly, and you will infuse ichor into the veins of the nation, and endow it with the immortality to which all Parliamentary countries are heirs.

That is the contention of one set of people whose faith is strong enough to move the Hæraus Mountains from their base and toss them into the North Atlantic.

Young Turkey's Aggressive Nationalism

Other publicists and statesmen see little to scandalise or repel them in the secrecy and irresponsibility of the Turkish Camorra. But they are disagreeably impressed by the narrow nationalist tendencies of the new régime and by the wild haste with which the present rulers of the country are seeking to turn Greeks into Turks, and gather figs from thistles. And the advice which these friends of Turkey offer sounds wholesome enough: "Do not try to denationalise in a year all the peoples that make up your population. Move slowly. Let assimilation be your ideal, if you will, but do not make it the immediate aim of your policy. In time, by dint of suasion and good treatment, you may perhaps Turkify your Greeks and Arabs, your Bulgars and Albanians, and call it Ottomanisation. But you must allow time for the process and use efficacious means. Violence will not win you love. And in no case can you accomplish the task by a decree in a twinkling. Meanwhile, shrink from embittering those peoples by threats and petty restrictions. On the contrary, humour them as much as possible, especially in little things. To attempt the impossible, as you have been doing hitherto, is to defeat your own object, to ruin a good cause, and to endanger the future of your country. Remember, that politics is the art of the possibly."

A third category of politicians discern Young Turkey's capital error in her extreme zeal for centralisation. The rulers of the nation want to do too much. They would fain grasp the unbounded, and they will be restless until they have bent the inflexible. Now they could not govern the empire and all its parts from Constantinople, and even if they could, it would be the height of wisdom to strip the nationalities of their Home Rule. "Under Abdul Hamid, centralisation was only formal. It existed on paper. In reality, the nationalities transacted their own business in their own ways. They enjoyed Home Rule. Your people were of a religion which made no difference among the nationalities that embraced it, and you caused the conquered races, in like manner, to transform themselves into religions. It was thus that Bulgars and Serbs and Kutzovlachs became Greeks by professing the orthodox faith. And Home Rule of a kind went with each recognised creed. Well, let those peoples go on governing themselves and preserving their national traits until you have men, money, and culture enough to relieve them of the burden. And even then, you will do well to leave them to their own devices so long as they work for the maintenance of the empire."

Young Turkey's Foreign Policy

There are other publicists and ministers of state who claim to have found the source of Turkey's present weakness and future reverses in her mistaken foreign policy. "She has begun to follow the wolf, not the shepherd," they affirm, "and she will have only herself to blame if she be eaten up at last. Abdul Hamid was an out-and-out Germanophile, and he ruined his country by giving the Kaiser a voice in his councils, and by bartering valuable concessions for worthless 'moral' support. The present good and wise sultan was, and is, of a different way of thinking. He would gladly follow the advice of Great Britain and France. When the present sultan was only Prince Imperial, he was wont to assure his few personal friends that he was a warm partisan of an alliance with England, and that he regarded the British nation as the only genuine friend of Turkey. That his brother should have taken up with Germany was to him a matter for profound regret. And as soon as he ascended the throne, England was regarded as the friend. Kiamil Pasha would not steer the ship of state towards German waters. Nor was it until Mahmoud Shefket Pasha came to the front and wielded dictatorial power that the engines were reversed."

"At first, the British Ambassador had all the trumps of the diplomatic game in his hand, and all the aces as well. That eminent diplomatist could not venture into the street without being followed by masses of enthusiastic men, who apotheosised him then and there until he resembled Mr Kipling's incarnation of Krishna. The German Ambassador, crestfallen and forsaken, was but as a broken idol compared to this powerful god. It was a splendid position for Great Britain: the sultan, the cabinet, the Young Turkish party, and the masses on her side, and an ambassador who had but to use ordinary common sense to keep the position thus come to him and his nation as a windfall."

Young Turkey Becomes Germanophile

"The events of April 13, 1909, and the quiescence of the ambassador changed all that. Mahmoud Shefket Pasha assumed dictatorial power as the friend and protégé of Germany, and he at once made room for his friend and protectress."

"Mahmoud Shefket had for years represented Turkey at the works of Krupp at Essen, where he was commissioned to watch over the execution of orders given by the Porte for artillery, &c., and to examine the materials before accepting delivery. And during this sojourn in Germany, he learned to appreciate his hosts, to whom he has been devotedly attached ever since. For Mahmoud Shefket is a brilliant warrior, and he feels drawn towards the one great militarist power in Europe. Owing to his influence, to that of the German Pasha, von der Goltz, and also to British diplomacy, Turkey changed her policy radically and went over to the German camp. If it would benefit either Germany or Turkey to have a written convention, military or other, it is not Shefket who would refuse it. But Turkey will need money, and ever more and more money, which France would refuse, if it were obviously destined to strengthen the Triple or Quadruple Alliance. That is the main reason why no convention has been concluded."

"And the nationalities under a truly constitutional government would have joined hands and fraternised. Did they not help Mahmoud Shefket Pasha to overthrow the old sultan and re-establish the constitutional system? Were not Greeks, Armenians, Turks, and Bulgars brothers, during the first revolution and for a long time afterwards? Peace and progress like this would have been worth more to the Turkey of today than the most brilliant victory over the Albanians or the Arabs. But the military party in Constantinople cannot, or will not, see it."

Those are some of the principal theories by which political writers explain to themselves and their readers the present situation in Turkey, and the outlook in the future, there. There is, of course, something to be said for each of them, and that alone is enough to show that no one of these explanations is adequate.

Why Young Turkey Cannot Last

My own view of the Turkish revolution, and the chances of a new state arising on the site of the old, has been constant. Having studied the question on the spot and having had the advantage of hearing Kiamil Pasha, Hakki Pasha, Cherif Pasha, Prince Sabah Eddin, and the chiefs of the various parties and groups state their views and define their aims, I went to the chiefs of the nationalities, to the (Ecumenical Patriarch, to the Armenian Patriarch, &c., &c.,) and discussed the matter with them in detail. Everything I heard and saw there, and during my subsequent visits, confirmed the belief I had from the very first, that the revolution was an attempt to reconcile two contradictories. It was an endeavour to join 'Yes' and 'No'; to combine snow with fire. Therefore, it could no more succeed than an attempt to bail out the water of the ocean with a fork. The difficulties which the régime heretofore encountered, and the obstacles that have risen on its way, may or may not be surmounted, but the upshot will be the same. The terms of the problem exclude a solution. Whether, if there had been other men at the helm, men like, say, Prince Sabah Eddin and Cherif Pasha, the problem could have been formulated differently, is another matter. As things were and are, Young Turkey is, in my opinion, a contradiction in terms, a chimera which cannot live. And whether the committee men abandon their game of hide-and-seek, accept office and govern constitutionally; whether they give up their scheme of rigorous centralisation; whether they moderate their fury against the nationalities and refrain from rendering the use of the Latin alphabet penal in Albania, and whether they turn their backs upon Germany and wend their way towards France and England, are all matters of no consequence so far as the final result is concerned.

Julius Caesar, Oliver Cromwell, and Napoleon III, were it possible to combine their genial powers to the best possible advantage, would toil in vain at the task of shifting the huge fabric of Islam, which is nothing if not religious, and placing it on a purely political groundwork, in the year of grace 1911. A miracle of transubstantiation would be needed, which is inconceivable today. In order to form even a faint and faraway notion of what the problem is like, let the reader take some concrete illustration on a small scale. The Jesuit Order offers an illustration. Everybody can imagine how powerful it is, or was in the heyday of its prosperity. What made the strength of that wonderful body of men? A religious idea which rendered all nationalities that embraced it brothers. The Chinaman, the Negro, the Spaniard, and the Englishman became, in truth, brothers, once they were admitted to the membership of the Order, which fused all nationalities, all class differences, all mental and physical in-equalities, and created one living organism, informed by a religious idea, inflamed by a fanatical spirit. Suppose for a moment that somebody among them were to propose that they should transform themselves into a purely political association for the purpose of attaining purely political aims without any reference to religion, what would people think of the would-be transformer? They would probably think him mad. But imagine for a moment that this enterprising spirit, going further, were to insist that the Jesuits should admit to membership, and treat as brethren, the heretics and schismatics whom it was their main purpose to convert to Catholicism; how would that sound as a practical proposal?

Well, it was a kindred scheme on an enormous scale, and bristling with incomparably more formidable difficulties, that the Young Turks set themselves to realise when they deposed the caliph, abandoned the precepts of the Koran, proclaimed the transformation of Islam into a political community, and conferred '*membership*' upon the giaours whom every pious Moslem had been taught to despise when he did not exterminate, for Turkey had never been a national community yet. It was a creed, and, like Catholicism and Buddhism, an international religion, which distinguished individuals by their religious beliefs only, not by their nationality. Neither had it ever been a political association. Turkey, the Turkey of all the sultans down to Abdul Hamid, was a religious community which ruled other religious communities – the Greek, the Armenian, the Bulgarian – which it conceived of only as creeds, not as nationalities. That such a religious body cannot be transmuted in a twinkling into a political state is evident. Yet the Young Turks have been acting on the supposition that it could be thus metamorphosed, and that they themselves had accomplished the fact.

The problem, it seems to me, is not soluble.

Wanton Cruelty of the Young Turks

And if over and above this internal difficulty, which I take to be insurmountable, others are added, such as hatred provoked by wanton cruelty – the cruelty which has been for ages inculcated by Islam – towards Christians, this artificial amalgam of nations and creeds, which is being temporarily kept together, may come to an end soon and suddenly. And here, the Young Turks have been extremely ill-advised from the first. The massacre of the Armenians at Adana is set down as one of the darkest blots on Young Turkey's scutcheon – and rightly. Hanging men in the streets of Constantinople for political opinions is another. The barbarous repression inaugurated in Albania by Torghut Pasha is a third. To these might be added the murders of Bulgarians, Macedonians, Greeks, and Serbs, who have been done to death with the old religious fury which is as prevalent as ever. To me, however, one of the characteristic traits of the Young Turks is their cruelty to animals, which in politics does not come into consideration at all. But it is surely a fair test of culture. And when one reads of the tens of thousands of dogs (the number has been given at 270,000) transported to an island in the Sea of Marmora and left there to perish slowly of hunger, one cannot think very highly of the authors of this method of ridding the capital of its four-footed scavengers.

Young Turkey's mode of action in Albania is not merely indefensible, it is inexplicable. Under Abdul Hamid, the Albanians were the most devoted friends of the Turks. The sultan's trusty guard was composed of men of this nationality. And the wily old monarch knew how to humour them. His successors turned a new leaf. Repression is their one panacea. They forbade the use of the Latin alphabet for the Albanian language, prescribing the Turkish, which is wholly unsuited to express the Albanian sounds with precision. They took irksome measures to get the Albanians to learn Turkish, which is a mixture of Ottoman, Persian, and Arabic, and has no literature worth reading. The Albanians resented this meddling in their home affairs. The relations between Turk and Albanian grew tense in consequence. Friction engendered heat, which soon burst into flame. Torghut Pasha was sent with troops to put down the insurrection. His savage cruelty won for him an unenviable name that will live for some generations to come. He put to death friend and enemy without discrimination, so long as they were both Albanians. Meanwhile, the secret government sent emissaries to Albania with the mission to turn the Christian Albanians against their Moslem fellow countrymen and foster feuds between them. This was a corollary of their aggressive nationalist policy. But it failed of its purpose. The Albanians held together, because one and all they are resolved to preserve their language and their national customs intact.

Loyal Albania Was Driven to Revolt

From influential Albanians, I heard that they cherished no separatist desires whatever. They were, and intended to remain, loyal to the Turks. I saw a letter from one of the chiefs, stating that he and others had given emphatic assurances to this effect. But the Young Turks received these statements with scepticism. Yet the Albanians are truthful and keep their promises. One cannot say as much of those Turks who have had dealings with them. More than once, the Young Turks have pledged their faith to the Albanian chiefs and broken it. One of these chiefs, named Zetir [Zeqir] – of the Krassnick clan – has over and over again declared that he would not accept the word of a Turk after his own experience during Torghut Pasha's expedition. Zetir's [Zeqir's] predecessor and uncle, Shaban Binak, was a partisan of the Turks and had sided with them. Yet immediately after the fighting in the Katchanik Pass, the Turks hanged him. Another Albanian notable, Hadji Russta, also a friend of the Turks, helped them actively against the famous Issa Boletinatz [Isa Boletini] last year. Him too, however, they seized and hanged the other day. What the Albanians resent most of all is the violation of the sacred bess [besa], or oath, which was committed in the case of Shaban Binak, whom the Young Turks invited to negotiate, having first sworn not to harm him, and when he was within their lines, they put him to death without trial or accusation. And now, Issa Boletinatz [Isa Boletini], Suleiman Aga Batoush, Zetir [Zeqir], and several other Albanian chieftains simply refuse to take the word of a Turk. And this result is worse than a reverse in the Albanian highlands. Under these circumstances, it is amusing to read in the Turkish Press criticisms on the 'equivocal attitude' of Issa Boletinatz [Isa Boletini]. In reality, his attitude springs from mistrust and is characterised by caution.

The impartial outsider will lay most of the blame for the rebellious behaviour of the Albanians on the inquisitorially oppressive misrule of the Young Turks, their provocative brutality, and their bad faith. Albania was as loyal to Turkey as Ulster is to England. But even this attachment, which resembled that of the Scottish Highlander of yore to the chieftain of his clan, was at last turned into active resistance. Even then, however, they were not fighting for separation but for those secular rights of theirs which would enable them to keep actively loyal in the future as in the past. That was the true meaning of the rising of the Malissores last spring. Many of them had been burned or smoked out of their own country by Torghut Pasha and had taken refuge in Montenegro. They were impatient for revenge, but their appeal to arms was premature, for the Shale and Shoshe [Shoshi] clans who would have joined them had no arms. About 1,300 of these had journeyed to Podgoritsa in Holy Week to petition the Montenegrins to supply them with rifles and ammunition. But the government of King Nicholas turned a deaf ear to their supplications, whereupon they returned empty-handed. And now before they could obtain arms, the five Malissore tribes raised the standard of rebellion and took the field. Issa Boletinatz [Isa Boletini] was sorely grieved, but he, too, was powerless. The Moslem Albanians, who dwell in Old Servia, would gladly have swelled the ranks of the insurgents, if the latter had waited a fortnight or three weeks longer, until the thaw had come and gone. But at the moment when the insurrection broke out on the borders of Montenegro, the mountains were still impassable from the snowdrifts, and the Mohammedan clans of Old Servia were constrained to remain at home inactive[9].

Russia's Diplomatic Note: The Why and Wherefore

Montenegro has Albanians of its own – the four clans, Kuchi, Orakhovo, Zatrievatz, and Fundina, who are related to and connected by marriage with the Turkish Albanians of the Klementi [Kelmendi] and Gruda clans. Hence, it is practically impossible for King Nicholas' government to keep them from snatching up their rifles – when they hear Turkish bullets whizzing by them – and rushing over the frontiers to the assistance of their brothers and cousins. This nearness of the clans, and the fact that the fighting has been taking place on the very frontiers, explain the accusations levelled against Montenegro. But both Montenegro and Russia have done their best to localise the struggle and keep the fire from

---

[9] Cf. *Novoyt Vremya*, June 3, 1911.

extending over the Peninsula. Russia's note to Turkey and her exhortations to Montenegro were moves in this direction. The intention in the former case was manifestly excellent, the form alone was defective, and this defect was intensified by the publication in a semi-official paper in St Petersburg of a text of the note before the Russian Ambassador in Constantinople had had time to see the Turkish Foreign Secretary. That was a grave technical blunder, but it does not vitiate the intention, nor do away with the necessity of taking action.

The truth is that Russia had to do something. For the Turks, whose troops were massed on the Montenegrin frontiers, were firing over the border into King Nicholas' territory. They themselves had admitted this. Nay, they announced that they could not well avoid it, and they hoped that the Montenegrins would not construe such action as overt acts of warfare. Now the Montenegrins are warriors first and men afterwards, and whenever they are in doubt as to who is the enemy, they have been taught to shoot the Turk, for he is the permanent enemy, and bullets spent on him are never wasted. Would it be possible to restrain such men and their friends the resident Albanians if the Turks were permitted to send volleys over the frontier? King Nicholas' ministers thought not. Accordingly, they requested Torghut Pasha's lieutenants to abstain from this dangerous practice, and at the same time, they appealed to Russia for counsel and diplomatic aid. It was then, and only then, that the St Petersburg Foreign Office decided to offer its advice to both parties, and if the intention had been carried out in a correct diplomatic way, all would have been well. But 'somebody blundered'.

Enter Austria-Hungary

Austria-Hungary took the next step. And whatever may be thought of the part which rivalry with Russia may have had among the considerations that moved Count Aehrenthal to action, it is undeniable that Austria's desire for peace and her traditional interest in the welfare of the Catholic Albanians, whom Turkish misrule had driven to revolt, offer adequate explanations for a step which was at once correct and salutary. An inspired article appeared in the press organ of the Austrian Foreign Office, stating that Franz Josef's advisers had repeatedly exhorted the Young Turks to conciliate the Albanians, in lieu of subduing them. It also contained this noteworthy judgment: "It is a matter for regret that the Turkish Government regards its task in Albania only as a brutal conquest of the insurgents...The present policy will culminate in impossible conditions." Those words, it seems to me, express adequately the significant fact that the Young Turks are fired by the same spirit, drawn towards the same goal, as their nomadic ancestors: "Conquer, exterminate, but do not trouble to build up. The state has no independent existence; it is an aspect of Islam, nothing more. When implicit obedience to the caliph is established, everything else will take care of itself."

At first, people rubbed their eyes and asked whether it was really the press organ of the Austrian Foreign Office that had brought out this spirited article. In Germany, especially, the publicists, who are supposed to hear the grass grow in Austria, were dismayed.

Warnings were uttered that if Austria-Hungary wants German support, she must concert her action with Germany in advance. Others were of the opinion that a merit should be made of necessity, and Count Aehrenthal's action should be supported by Herr von Kiderlen Waechter. From all these discussions and criticisms, one fact emerges very distinctly. It is this: the Albanian problem tends to become a European issue and has already set the Great Powers moving. Another thing which, however, is more of a deduction is, that Young Turkey is seen by Europe to be incapable of carrying on the business of the empire without help from without. Today, she needs advice, admonition, and money.

Later on, unless the money keeps flowing in from outside, she may need military support as well.

The Conquering Hero Comes Too Late

Austria's counsel could not be ignored. It was agreed to adopt it at the eleventh hour. Sultan Mohmmood, who was about to commence his journey to Macedonia, which had been announced a long while before, was authorised by his government to carry an olive branch for the rebellious Albanians in the form of an amnesty. Great hopes were based upon this act of clemency. It would touch the hearts of the chivalrous highlanders and combine with the scenic display, to remind the Albanians that there still lives a sultan in Turkey who has money to spend and favours to accord. Nor was it only the common men who were to be pardoned. The ringleaders would also be included in the list of the forgiven. In a word, the plan was well laid, as Turkish plans go, but like so many other well-laid schemes, it went 'agley'. A new dramatis persona entered on the scene.

The Catholic Mirdites are a clan which is, without being very numerous, warlike, compact, dauntless. It is admirably well organised. The number of men it can put into the field is computed variously. I am disposed to set it down at about ten thousand men. But they are a resourceful body of warriors. Last year, when Torghut Shefket Pasha 'trampled out the insurrection', these rebels were disarmed by force and by fraud. Yet this year, they have managed to arm themselves anew in some mysterious way and to hoist the standard of insurrection. This time, they have disclaimed the moderate aims which they pursued last year. They are no longer fighting for the mere status quo as it was under Abdul Hamid; they have come to the conclusion that even this minimum of demands will never be granted to them without Home Rule. Separation from Turkey is what they now ask for. "It is as easy to break an oath three and four times as twice," one of their leaders remarks, and he infers that no amnesty and no fair words are acceptable as a solution. Ever since April last, I have been aware of the intention of the Albanians to ask for separation, and I also learned something more of the genesis of this resolve and of the ways and means by which it was proposed to carry it out. But I must confess, I expected to see earlier signs of the execution than this proclamation made in the second decade of June. And when it became known that the sultan *of* Turkey was empowered to proclaim an amnesty, to authorise the Albanians to carry arms as in the old days, and to use the Latin alphabet, I felt some doubt whether the cry for separation would ever be raised. But the two incidents have coincided in time.

Autonomy for Albania

Terenzio Tocchi, a personal friend of Ricciotti Garibaldi's and said to be a member of one of the Albanian colonies in Italy, has proclaimed himself president of the provisional Albanian Government. I saw a copy of a letter the other day which Ricciotti Garibaldi gave him, to Italians in America, when he crossed the Atlantic some time ago. The news of the proclamation was received in Constantinople with indifference. Shefket Torghut Pasha would take the rising as one of the items of his day's work and settle it satisfactorily, the Young Turks said. He certainly has already brought the military expedition within sight of the goal. The theatre of operations is narrowed down to a small area. The insurgents are cut off from several roads indispensable to successful strategic moves on their part. They cannot take refuge in Montenegro, because Shefket Torghut's troops stand between them and the frontier. And now, they have no way of obtaining provisions, we are told. Accordingly, their number is dwindling rapidly. A week or so more, say Turkish optimists, and the Mirdites will be reduced to a similar plight, whereupon it will be much easier to talk reason with the malcontents. Such was the Turkish view at the outset.

In Vienna, a different feeling prevailed. The insurrection of the Mirdites would, it was pointed out by the Neue Freie Presse, necessitate further Turkish reinforcements. Shefket Torghut would have to dispatch a part of his corps of operations and endanger his success in Northern Albania. Moreover, the Turks could not find any such suitable base for operations against the Mirdites, as they have had in Skutari against the other rebels. Add to this, the circumstance that the land inhabited by the Mirdites is uncommonly favourable to a warlike tribe carrying on a guerrilla struggle against regular troops. Unhappily, the contest will be fiercest on the very border of Montenegro, and it will become increasingly difficult to hold back King Nicholas' bellicose subjects, who, after all, are men of flesh and blood of whom it may be said with truth that however willing the spirit may be, the flesh is very weak. It looks today as though the matter were ripe for Europe. Montenegro is already preparing for the worst and has ceased to hope for the best. Austria-Hungary is on the alert. Italy is growing aggressively neutral. And Russia is biding her time.

If the Albanians were to receive autonomy from the powers, things in Turkey would soon come to a head. True, if only a few Catholic clans in the North obtained self-government, the consequences would not be serious. But if, as Terenzio Tocchi hopes, the Albanians as a single people were recognised by Europe as autonomous, it would connote the beginning of the end for Young Turkey. The influential Vienna journal, Neue Freie Presse, affirms that in this case the Sandjak of Novibazar would, so to say, be suspended in mid-air, seeing that the Mohammedan Albanians inhabit Old Servia right up to the frontiers of the Servian Kingdom, and only here and there do groups of Serbs come in as wedges between them. Whether this contingency of autonomy is realised or not, the circumstance that it is become a contingency offers an apt illustration of the political incapacity of the Young Turks and of the practical impossibility of welding the peoples and creeds of the Ottoman Empire into political homogeneity. A while ago, the Albanians were more Turkish in spirit than the Young Turks themselves. Yet they have been so harassed and persecuted by systematic attempts to denationalise them, and so incensed by the inhuman methods employed to overcome their resistance, that in the short space of two years they have become dangerous enemies of the new régime.

E. J. Dillon

The Contemporary Review, July–December 1911

Roumania and Albania

Roumania, it may be objected, will exert her moral influence, and if necessary, her military power, to hinder the outbreak or neutralise the result of a Balkan war, this being one of the functions which her position as chief of the petty states imposes on her. And the remark is true, but it has its limitations. Countries live first for themselves, and only afterwards, and in a much less degree, for their neighbours, and it is conceivable – nay, to my thinking, probable – that Roumania will have burning problems of her own to solve before the present decade has run even half its course. And of these, the agrarian and electoral reforms are not only the most arduous but also the most perturbing. The exertion needed *to* carry these may immobilise the forces, financial and military, of the realm for several years, and compel the government to content itself with a less active role in the conduct of foreign affairs than it contemplates today. A veritable revolution from above is being prepared in Roumania, and although the authorities will themselves choose the moment and set the machine in motion, it is by no means certain that they will always be able to regulate its rate of progress or circumscribe the limits of its operation. From the ensuing ordeal, a new

Roumania will emerge, concerning which it is premature to make any predictions. Democracy will assert its claim to rule there, and it is certain that the views of the masses on the relations that ought to subsist between the country and its neighbours differ widely from those which obtained for the past thirty-five years.

That is one aspect of the Balkan problem which most people forget to allow for in their forecasts of what is coming.

Another element that has to be reckoned with Albania. No one knows what to expect from that gifted people when once it is allowed to govern itself. That Slav neighbours should augur ill of the new political creation which stands between them and the sea is natural, and their prophecies are veritable lamentations. The ministers of King Nicholas of Montenegro recently impressed upon me the necessity of whittling down Albania as much as possible, not only in the interests of Europe and of peace but also of Albania herself! No European Conference, they argued, can so regulate the mutual relations between Albania and Montenegro as to safeguard peace. Austria's plan, as put forward in London, is sure to be a fruitful source of quarrels and conflicts between the two peoples. And the war which may at any moment result may involve their respective protectors.

These arguments are easily answered. But as they have no effect upon those to whom they are addressed, it is needless to analyse them here. Albania, to be viable at all, should be strong. But the stronger she is strategically and the more territory – occupied by men of Albanian stock – she possesses, the greater her chance of surviving the trials to which during the next few decades she is certain to be exposed. Whether it was wise or foolish to create an independent Albania is an idle question. But once the resolution was taken, everything possible should have been done to render the new nation self-supporting in every respect. The idea that the Albanians are incapable of self-government is absurd. They are better qualified for it than a certain European state which is now floundering about in chaotic ooze under a so-called democratic government. True, in the north there are tribes whose manners and customs are mediaeval and barbarous. But even they are richly endowed with developed, and also embryonic, qualities that render them amenable to good government and susceptible of the highest forms of culture. Moreover, the manner in which this curious political experiment is being tried commands the approval of statesmen who have no axe of their own to grind.

Albanian Characteristics

In the new autonomous organisation, there will, I am told, be no state religion. The administration will be organised in one part of the realm in accordance with ancient Albanian customs and traditions, and in another, in harmony with Turkish laws. Western civilisation will, of course, be grafted on the new political organisation, but due care will be taken not to force the note. The character of the people, their likes and dislikes, cannot be changed overnight, and one must not expect figs from thorns. In all probability, in spite of strong objections both to Valona and Durazzo as the capital because of the ease with which they could be attacked from the sea, Ismail Kemal Bey advocates the choice of the former while several of his political opponents favour the latter town. The argument in favour of a small Albania which Montenegro draws from the danger of war breaking out between the two countries is not convincing, inasmuch as Albania will be a neutral state. At the outset, it will have no regular army, only a gendarmerie. But the gendarmes will consist of three different corps, infantry, cavalry, and artillery, and will thus form the nucleus of what, in time, will doubtless become the regular army.

That the Albanians are behind the times, benighted and superstitious, is notorious, although very few of those writers who depreciate them are aware to what extent this is true. In the northern districts, a bad man is believed to become a lugat, a sort of ghoul, after his death. He visits his relations at night and perpetrates all manner of unpleasant freaks to worry or damage them and then returns to his grave and recommences his tricks the next night. If a white stallion refuses to jump a grave, that is a sure sign that the dead man has become a lugat. The inhabitants thereupon fill up the grave with dry twigs and boughs, saturate them with petroleum, and set fire to the mass. That fire annihilates the lugat. If, however, this operation is put off too long, it becomes inefficacious, because in the meanwhile the lugat has been transformed into a kukuth and is thenceforward a scourge of mankind generally. Phosphorescence over a grave is an indication of sanctity.

Between Yagodina and Berat, the huts are made of dung, straw, and rafters. The Rivers Semani and Vyosse [Vjosa] submerge every year more than 15,000 hectares of land, and for lack of bridges, traffic is often suspended for weeks at the time when the flocks are returning from the pastures. The shepherds then seek out a ford, and one of them, holding a bell which he keeps continuously ringing, leads the way, while his comrades cross lower down the stream, form themselves into a chain across the water and endeavour to catch whatever animals are swept away by the current. Three-fourths of the population are victims of infectious diseases[10]. The hospitality of the people is unparalleled. They go to quixotic lengths in their respect for the guest whom circumstance has brought under their roof. An instance which came to the personal knowledge of a cultured Albanian whom I know, named Ekrem Bey Vlora, is worth recording. My acquaintance was the guest of one of his own countrymen when, in the dead of night, the corpse of the host's son was carried home. He had fallen a victim to vendetta. And the host ordered the members of his family, who were wild with grief, to abstain from moaning and sobbing lest their guest should be disturbed in his sleep!

It is impossible to converse with Albanians of mark, like, say, MM. Nogga and Konitza, without feeling favourably impressed towards the nation to which they belong. And this impression is strengthened by the circumstance that the country, although devoid of police and without a properly organised government, is perfectly tranquil and the prisons empty at a moment when disorder bordering on chaos is widespread in the neighbouring kingdoms. This may be taken as proof that the Albanian people are well-fitted to look after their own affairs.

I have discussed the future of Albania time and again with the most prominent men of the nation, including, of course, the provisional head of the government, Ismail Kemal, whose diplomatic finesse would have done honour to the statesmen of Florence in the days of the Medicis. Some of these politicians have been accused of taking money bribes from

---

[10] Cf. Ekrem Bei Vlora. Aus Berat und vom Tomor, Sarajevo.

Italy, Austria, and Turkey, and possibly from other states as well. Whether and to what extent this charge is grounded is a matter with which I am not now concerned. But, assuming it to be true, one has to envisage the subject from an Albanian, not a European, point of view, and to judge the accused from a standard wholly different from that which would apply to British, French, or German public men of today. The Albanian will take a bribe without the slightest qualm, and his countrymen will never think of withdrawing their confidence or esteem from him on that account. They deem the procedure natural, for money is but an outward sign that talent is discerned and appreciated. Nothing more. Gratitude from the recipient is not to be expected and is never given. Indeed, the word thanks connotes a state of feeling which, presumably, is never experienced by an Albanian. In this connection, I remember an interesting incident that occurred some years ago in Athens. An Albanian poet presented some excellent verses of his to Queen Olga of Greece, who, among other accomplishments, possesses a fair knowledge of that curious old tongue. Her Majesty sent for the author and said: "I cannot offer you my thanks for your admirable verses which I read and enjoyed, for there is no word for thanks in Albanian, but I read your poems with much interest and was quite pleased." The nearest approach to the phrase 'I thank you' is 'I am contented'. And an Albanian who receives a gratuity from a foreign government is merely contented, nothing more. He does not feel in the slightest degree obliged to do anything in return. He never sells his country or his country's interests.

E. J. Dillon

The Contemporary Review, October 1911

Albanian Characteristics

Albania has thus become the powder magazine of the Balkans, whereas it possesses all the makings of a little state more prosperous, better ordered, and more efficiently defended than Montenegro. The country is fertile. Large tracts of forest land contain the best timber to be found in Europe – secular trees which cannot be matched between the Balkan Peninsula and California. Various minerals, excellent tobacco, olives, vines, and in two districts naphtha, give promise of future economic well-being. But they call for systematic exploitation, which is still impossible. The people, too, are extremely docile, and, when skilfully taken in hand, faithful and devoted. Turkish misrule, endured for ages, has left its mark on their habits and ways of thought. From the military angle of vision, they are in their element as sharpshooters and in guerrilla warfare, whereas in the open field they are easily disconcerted and almost useless. Thievishness, especially in the mountaineers, has become almost second nature. I was once in the hills among two hundred chiefs of clans all armed to the teeth. Struck with the suppleness of their movements and the ease with which they handled their rifles, I uttered a few words of praise to their feudal lord. "Ah, yes," he answered, "they are splendid fellows. They are capable of taking an impregnable position and the shirt off your back with equal dexterity. All my men are past masters in the art of thieving." Manual labour has less attraction for them. Unaccustomed to work, they cannot be expected to learn in this generation. Their sons may be trained to toil for their living, but that the fathers should turn their rifles into harrows or ploughshares is out of the question. Field work and manual labour generally fall to the lot of the women.

The vendetta is a custom which is ingrained in the Albanian temperament and cannot be done away with by the waving of the lawgiver's wand. In a land without a code of recognised criminal law or a body of police, every male has to fall back upon the principles of natural law and defend himself as best he can with firearms or cold steel. And vendetta is a rude effort to codify and idealise the custom by hedging it around with conditions and suspending it during important conjunctures when larger interests are at stake – as, for instance, during an incursion by the Montenegrins or a punitive expedition of the Turks. So long as Albania was ruled from Stamboul, the sultan's officials fostered the custom and egged on the dilatory to be revenged on their enemies. For according to the unwritten law, every man who killed his enemy had to pay blood money for the deed. The price per life varied from thirty-five to sixty Turkish pounds, and as the vendetta was an affair of honour indispensable to the very existence of a large group of kinsmen, the money was always accurately paid. About one-third of the sum went to the Ottoman Government, and the remainder was distributed among the relatives of the victim.

In the case of Prenk Bib Doda, of Kalmetty [Kallmeti], and his forbears and descendants, the Sublime Porte dispensed with this blood tax, leaving its own share to the chieftain of the Mirdites himself. And it is still one of the perquisites today.

Time, endeavour, understanding, tact, and money employed by a ruler who, besides being a free agent, should be gifted with resourcefulness and will power, would weld those materials together and build up a viable state, if only hindrances from without were withdrawn. The feudal system, in lieu of impeding the work, would facilitate it if properly handled and fully utilised.

A religious problem in the European sense can hardly be said to exist, and one could keep it from cropping up by treating the Mohammedans with justice and fairness, which they are not slow to appreciate. Religious strife has been hitherto unknown in Albania. Much more difficult is the task of inuring to labour a people whose main occupations are war, smoking, coffee-drinking, and basking in the sun. Hardly less arduous is the obstacle to progress offered by the Young Albanians, who are already the nucleus of a small political party which would fain transform the country and the people overnight, abolish secular customs, pull down the feudal framework of society, redistribute the land, found a national University and an Academy of Letters, and inaugurate for their regenerate countrymen an era of well-being and progress. Unhappily, these would-be reformers have a programme calculated to draw a considerable following. When there are spoils to be gathered, there are freebooters near. "Open a cask of sugar," says an Eastern proverb, "and the flies will come even from Baghdad." But haste of this kind in Albania is the forerunner of disaster.

Benighted Condition of the Albanian People

The depths of ignorance in which the bulk of the Albanians are plunged can hardly be fathomed by the Western. One or two concrete instances will enable the reader to form a faint and faraway idea of their benighted condition. Prenk Bib Doda, the hereditary chief of the Mirdites, after having passed most of his life in exile, was suddenly permitted to return to his people in the year 1909, if I remember right. His tribesmen rejoiced exceedingly when the tidings were brought to them, for they expected that the pasha's arrival would usher in an era of peace and plenty, and his reign would be that of a Messiah. When time had cooled their ardour and reality had turned their hopes to disillusion, they spoke harshly of their chief and found fault with his acts. It was whispered among them that he had become a Turk in Stamboul and had forfeited the right to rule the clan. To those who assured them that Bib Doda was as good a Catholic as themselves, they turned a deaf ear. "But we know he is a Moslem," they insisted, "only of course he dissembles it because he dares not let it be known."

"How do you know? Have you any proof?"

"Certainly, we have. We have witnesses, eye-witnesses who are ready to swear that he washes his feet every day!" On another occasion, the conversation turned upon France. "Who is their 'King'?" asked the Mirdites.

"They have none. France is a 'Republic'."

"What's that?" they inquired. The answer, given in clear, detailed, and simple language, evoked no corresponding idea in the hearers' brains. It was then paraphrased with homely illustrations but to no purpose. One might as well talk to a blind man of colours. "Had the French never a king then?"

"Yes, over a hundred years ago."

"Well, in that case his son was king after him, and his grandson after that."

"Not so, for they beheaded their king."

"No, no, that can never be," they objected. "A king is made by God, and nobody can touch him, no matter what he may do. That is not possible. There must be a king in France!"

From the spirit that prompted those questions and comments, one can form a notion of the absolute power which the chieftains exercise over their tribesmen, and also of the obstacles which this ancient institution may, if rashly handled, place in the way of a political and social transformation. This feudal authority is indispensable to the new sovereign, but how to appropriate it without upsetting the system and precipitating a revolution is the Sphinx riddle which the Prince zu Wied has to solve. He tried his hand on Essad Pasha, his war minister, a man of means and influence, who was alleged to be plotting against him, but the method of his agents, the Dutch officers, was so incredibly clumsy that they turned the suspect into a hero, sent him into exile, and exhibited the sovereign in a role which bereft him of his prestige. Essad's house was bombarded at night, he and his dependents were arrested, and he was shipped off to Italy without being charged with any criminal overt act. And this unjustifiable act was done in the name of the Christian ruler.

The next piece of bungling was perpetrated in dealing with a number of Mohammedan villagers who had been taught by emissaries to believe that their religion was in danger and their hopes of prosperity blasted by a Christian prince. They were stung to fury by the sudden appearance of a contingent of armed Malissores in their midst, and a skirmish took place which, blood having been spilled, estranged them from their ruler, who, fearing a general massacre, took flight from his capital and sought asylum on board an Italian warship. The authors of this folly were also the Dutch officers, who put in the plea of good intentions. And they are undoubtedly well-intentioned, hard-working, and conscientious men. But with the sole exception of Colonel Thomson, who has rendered real services to Albania, their influence on the affairs of Albania has been pernicious.

Albania's Strong Man

But even the most useful agencies cannot be other than baneful when they set themselves to baulk each other's well-meant efforts. Too many cooks spoil the broth. And Albania suffers from a plethora of political advisers who dissent from each other on nearly every matter of moment, forgetting that Albanian politics are, in last analysis, European, and move in such vast circles, that none of the actors in the Durazzo drama can measure them with an arc long enough to determine their entire curve. Two men, however, deserve honourable mention, Turkhan Pasha and Phillip Nogga, the former a Nestor and Ulysses in one, one of the cleverest diplomatists and most fascinating talkers in Europe, and the other the soul of such stable progress in the country as has already begun to manifest itself to the close observer. Turkhan Pasha's services consist less in what he has himself been able to achieve in the way of constructive work than in what he has kept others from doing in the matter of destruction. He has maintained peace and prevented discord among his colleagues, remedied grievances before the complainants could become rebels, and extinguished sparks that bade fair to kindle consuming fires. Phillip Nogga is the man of the future, the culture-bearer of Albania, who has gauged with scientific precision the slow pace at which permanent progress is possible. He is ready to take his motive power wherever he may find it, from the Beys and Pashas, from the chieftains of clans, from the Malissores, the Catholic clergy, the Moslems and the Bek Tashi [Bektashi] Sectarians. Everything is grist that can be ground in his mill and employed for the benefit of his country. I have seen him at work day and night under most trying conditions, and I feel that I am stating the case moderately when I characterise him as the most Albanian of the ministers and the most active. He is wont to look before and after, and he sees further than anyone else. It was he who, amid discordant reports about the overwhelming strength of the rebels, set the number down at some four or five hundred and refused to believe that they would march on the capital. And events bore out his forecast. It was he who rushed to the palace and adjured the king to remain at his post on the historic Saturday, and it is he who has been keeping things going ever since. A man with many mental facets, he is wont to utter his opinions and proffer his advice to his sovereign with a plainness, directness, and pungency which enable him to make a profound, if not always a pleasant, impression. He knows his own mind, realises the limitations of circumstance, and has an invincible grasp of the principle of government as applicable to his countrymen. Alone, as sole minister without a cabinet, assisted by active subordinates chosen by himself, and freed from the guardianship of foreign commissions, he could, I believe, knead his countrymen into a tolerable political community.

M. Nogga is an opportunist. He has a political programme in petto, but he is careful to tackle only such parts of it as are feasible, to utilise opportunity as it offers, and to impart to all reforms the peculiar shape which alone will make them acceptable to the people for whose behoof they are undertaken. Only an Albanian can govern the Albanians with any hope of bending them to those beneficent but distasteful schemes of social and political transformation upon the realisation of which their destinies depend. Neither international Commissions of Control, nor Dutch officers, nor Italian and Austrian counsellors, can obtain for their reforms – if they have devised any scheme of reforms worthy of the name – access to the minds of the natives. His first postulate, therefore, is that Europe shall allow the natural leaders of the people a free hand to work out their destinies on the lines already approved by the powers and shall restrict the action of such international bodies as cannot yet be withdrawn to the functions for which they were created. And, to my mind, this measure is an indispensable condition of success. I may add that among the Albanians the only native whom I have yet met capable of bringing this arduous task to a good end is M. Nogga. Sureya Bey Vlora, the present minister in Vienna, is also a man of uncommon ability, self-esteem, and broad views, but as yet he has not had an opportunity of displaying his talents under the irritating conditions which at present obtain. On the contrary, he decided to serve his country abroad because he felt unable to make any headway at home until the obstacles which now block the way are displaced.

Austria and Italy in Albania

Between Italians and Austrians in Albania and their Press champions in Rome and Vienna, jars and bickerings have arisen which, while they do not contribute to augment the prestige of either side, have seriously embarrassed their respective governments. It would be unfruitful to dwell on them here or offer any remark beyond the expression of my belief that the pacific and tranquillising policy which each of these powers would fain pursue stands a much better chance of being carried out, the greater the freedom of action which they concede to the Albanians themselves. Nothing is easier or more noxious than to form a strong Italophile and an equally strong Austrophile party in the country, for the bulk of the Albanian people is ever ready to accept offerings from every source and for every purpose. Some of the principal chiefs have been for years in the pay of several powers which have nothing, as yet, to show for the expenditure. M. Nogga, when asked by Count Berchtold and the Marquis di San Giuliano what Austria-Hungary and Italy could do for his struggling countrymen, answered: "The most helpful thing would be to desist from distributing money among them, under any circumstances or for any purposes, however praiseworthy..." The request may yet be complied with. If Italy and Austria-Hungary could agree upon a self-denying ordinance to abstain from influencing the Albanian Government, once there is a real government in that country, Albania would have attained one of the indispensable conditions of regeneration.

The Origin and Aims of Italy's Foreign Policy

The problems with which Italian statesmen have for several decades been grappling are uncommonly difficult and delicate.

Probably no European Government has in recent times been confronted with a task so thorny as that with which the responsible advisers of the three kings of United Italy have had to deal. And the tact, resourcefulness, and suppleness with which they have achieved a set of results which theoretically seemed unattainable and incompatible with each other command the admiration of competent judges. Italy's foreign policy resembles nothing so much as one of those egg dances which Pope Leo X. delighted to witness after his Lucullan banquets. And the deftness and rapidity with which moves are made and steps taken that seem certain to crush this egg or that, yet do no damage to any of them, are amazing. But unlike the papal dancers, the statesmen of the consulta can look forward to no prize, to no popular applause. Abroad, they are accused of double-dealing, and at home of pursuing a costly policy of adventure. France charges them with ingratitude and perfidy. In Great Britain, they are sometimes set down as schemers. In Vienna, they are mistrusted, while Berlin indulges in scepticism or holds its judgment in suspense. And, to crown all, they are blamed or repudiated by a certain section of their own people, whose welfare they have been laboriously endeavouring to promote.

Italy's policy in its general lines has been imposed by circumstance and tempered by statesmanship. Far from embodying utopian notions or manifesting herself in dubious ventures, she has kept well within the limits of the essential, the indispensable. By making common cause with the two military powers of Central Europe and forming the Triple Alliance, she steered clear of a conflict with Austria-Hungary, which, so far as one can discern, there was no other way of avoiding. Italian irredentism in the Dual Monarchy and the rivalry of the two states in the Adriatic had confronted them both with the dilemma of choosing between a formal alliance and open antagonism. The decision took the form of a bold move but a necessary one. Italy's adherence to the league gave deep offence to France and led to their estrangement, which was followed by several Press campaigns and one damaging tariff war. And in spite of the subsequent reconciliation, the relations between the two Latin nations have never since been marked by genuine cordiality. The press of France and many eminent politicians there resent it as a sort of racial treason that Italy should be bound by treaty to Germany and Austria-Hungary. Russia, who for a time cultivated a close friendship with the Italian people, was surprised and pained by the seemingly needless and ostentatious renewal of the Triple Alliance in the year 1912, a twelvemonth before it had terminated. Even British publicists have found much to condemn in the attitude of the Italian Government during the Balkan War and down to the present moment. During all this time, the cultivation of rudimentary neighbourliness, to say nothing of friendship between the Italian and the Austrian peoples as distinguished from their governments, has been for the statesmen of both countries, and in particular for those of Rome, a work of infinite care, ingenious expedients, and painful self-discipline, openly deprecated by an influential section of the Italian Press.

The alpha and omega of Italy's foreign policy in the present is the maintenance of her actual position in the Mediterranean, and in the future, the seasonable improvement of that position, and in every case, the prevention of a shifting of the equilibrium such as would alter it to her disadvantage. To attain these objects is an essential condition of Italy's national existence and calls for the constant exercise of vigilance and caution alternating with push and daring by her responsible rulers. It behoves her, therefore, to be well affected towards France, friendly with Austria, amicable with Great Britain, to hold fast to the Triple Alliance, and to give no cause for umbrage to the Triple Entente. In a word, it is the prestidigitation of statesmanship. And her diplomacy has acquitted itself well of the task. The sum of the efforts of successive governments has been to raise Italy to a unique position in Europe, to make her a link between the two rival groups of powers, to one of which she herself belongs, to bestow upon her the second place in the Triple Alliance, and to invest her with enormous influence for peace in the councils of Europe. To grudge her this influence, which has been uniformly exerted for the best interests of Europe and her own, implies imperfect acquaintance with those interests, or else a leaning towards militarism. Every development which tends to strengthen Italy, diplomatically and politically, tends also to augment the safeguards of public peace, and to lessen the chances of a European conflict. On these grounds, therefore, were there none other, a violent domestic reaction against the policy that has scored such brilliant results, would be an international calamity. Happily, there is good hope that the bulk of the nation is wiser and also stronger than the section which is answerable for and in secret sympathy with the recent excesses.

Italy And Austria In the Adriatic

As the Mediterranean state par excellence, Italy cannot contemplate the present distribution of power on the shores of that sea with genuine complacency. The grounds for dissatisfaction are rooted in the history of her past and in her apprehensions for the future. Nonetheless, the status quo in Europe being hallowed must be respected under heavy pains and penalties. And the policy of the consulta is directed to its maintenance, because any modification of it in favour of another state, great or small, would infallibly drive Italy out of her quiescence and strain her to press with all her energies and at all risks in the direction of a favourable readjustment. That is why seventeen years ago, the Austrian and the Italian Foreign Secretaries concluded the so-called Noli Me Tangere Convention, by which each of the two allies undertook to abstain from meddling with Albania, to uphold Turkish rule there, and failing that to establish self-government. It was in virtue of the same principle that during the Balkan War Italy supported Austria-Hungary in frustrating Servia's attempt to divide up Albania among the allies and obtain for herself access to the Adriatic. As long as the Adriatic continues to present the same essential factors as today, the Italian Government will not swerve from its present attitude. But if once those factors or their relative positions towards each other underwent a change, the whole scaffolding of self-denial and everything that rested upon that would fall to pieces like a house of cards. And that scaffolding supports the peace of Europe.

On her Eastern shore, Italy possesses no port capable of serving as a thoroughly suitable base for naval operations. Brindisi is at best a mere makeshift; Venice is no better. Italy's rival, Austria, on the other hand, is luckier. Cattaro, Sebenico, and Pola serve the purpose admirably, giving the Austrian navy a distinct advantage in this respect. It must therefore be gall and wormwood to Italian politicians to think that an ideal port, Valona, on the Albanian coast, a few hours from Italy, lies unutilised because each state grudges it to the other on grounds which cannot be reasoned away. Valona, incorporated in the Habsburg Monarchy, which is already so well equipped on the Adriatic both for defence and attack, would turn the scale against Italy, upset the equilibrium which is at present accepted as a stern necessity, and might even unchain the forces of war. The prospect of kindred eventualities forbids Austria to allow that magnificent naval base to fall into the hands of her rival who, holding the key to the Adriatic, could close the Otranto Canal and immobilise the fleet of the Dual Monarchy.

It would be unfair, therefore, to contend that the mainspring of Italy's seemingly anti-Slav policy is racial bitterness or political narrow-mindedness. A natural instinct of self-preservation underlies it which neither argument nor sentiment can affect. Her present wish and the object of her endeavours is to enable Albania to maintain her independence and to keep the equilibrium in the Adriatic intact. And it is sheer inconceivable that any Italian Government should deviate from this line of action. If unforeseen events baulked these efforts and necessitated a partition of the newly founded state, Italy, like Austria-Hungary, would proceed to draw the practical consequences from the altered conditions, by such means as appeared most conducive to her interests. But it is by no means a foregone conclusion, as so many politicians and publicists fancy, that the exigencies of this new situation could be met only by an appeal to arms. This belief, which has become a dogma of political faith, is entirely gratuitous. Just as the jarring note which irredentism continually introduces into their mutual relations has not wholly marred the ground tones of harmony, so these potential differences – which cut far deeper into the vital interests of each – might be settled provisionally or definitively by some surprising combination such as has not as yet entered into the mind of any European statesman. For it should not be forgotten that the Triple Alliance is rooted in a peremptory necessity which is far more puissant than any of the centrifugal forces with which its individual members are beset. Failure to recognise this master fact of European politics has more than once lured statesmen on to abortive policies and perilous experiments.

It is entirely misleading, therefore, to assert that Italy's alliance with the two military powers of Central Europe is the result of eclectic affinities, or to fancy that by cajolery or threats she can be moved to sever the links that bind her to the concern. I entertain not the slightest doubt that the French Ambassador in Rome, M. Barère, whose infinite patience and marvellous tact drew France and Italy very close together for a while, would be the first to recognise that the breaking-up of the Triple Alliance is a hopeless enterprise, and an aim of questionable utility from any point of view. Outsiders, whose opinions are moulded by the daily press, may be excused for thinking otherwise. The renewal of the treaty in the year 1912, a full year before its expiry, has been uniformly construed as an indication of Italy's resolve to emphasise her friendship with her allies, and this interpretation appeared to be borne out by a number of concomitant circumstances and in particular by the comments of the European press. It was likewise assumed that at the same time the treaty was supplemented by a naval convention turning upon the future action of the Triple Alliance in the Mediterranean. I investigated these reports in Rome and elsewhere, and I received convincing evidence that they were both equally groundless. No new clause touching the naval forces of the alliance or indeed dealing with anything else was added to the treaty. It was renewed as it stood. And the early date at which it was signed was credibly explained to me as the outcome of a legitimate eagerness on the part of Italy to see reaffirmed by Austro-Hungary the noli me tangere convention which acted as a bar to encroachments, territorial or other, on Albania.

Italy, France, and Great Britain

Between France and Italy, the cordiality established mainly by the exertions of M. Barère has of late years undergone a marked change, and while the two governments were endeavouring to smooth over their differences and deal amicably with each contentious matter as it cropped up, the press of each country was bombarding the other with taunts and reproaches which rendered the task of diplomacy unnecessarily difficult. And British publicists for reasons which lie near the surface felt inclined to take sides with their French colleagues, without perhaps investigating with sufficient closeness and care the origin of the estrangement. Those unfriendly utterances, some of them the effects of mere misunderstandings, run through contemporary political history like a red thread through a piece of white cambric.

Italy's solicitude for friendship with France and Great Britain is prompted by interest as well as sentiment. For she sorely needs peace, recognises the need, and is exerting herself to the utmost to insure it. And this indisputable fact might profitably serve as the starting point of one's reasoning on the subject and likewise as a safe basis for the attitude of the statesmen interested. For a long time, it is true, the occupation of Tunis by France in 1887 was resented by every public man in the peninsula. The ensuing tension was accentuated as much by the manner as by the policy of Crispi. The Abyssinian campaign made matters worse, seeing that the Abyssinians were believed to have received their arms and ammunition from the French. During all those untoward incidents, Great Britain was found on Italy's side. The Franco-Italian war of tariffs raised mutual animosity to its highest power, after which a reaction set in which led to the conclusion of the Mediterranean agreements with France and England.

During the Lybian war, Italy seized two French steamers, the 'Manuba' and the 'Carthage', for alleged contravention of international law and sent them to Cagliari. France protested and M. Poincaré took up such a decided position in the matter and gave it such vehement expression that all Italy was unanimous in holding him up as the destroyer of the good relations laboriously established by M. Barère and the consulta. And the affront has not yet been forgotten. The next grievance had its source in the action of the British Government which confided to France the protection of her Mediterranean interests and encouraged the republic to keep the bulk of its warships in that sea. This preponderance of the French fleet in Italy's only sea was regarded by the government of the peninsula as an unfriendly act owing to its special bearings on their relative naval strength there. And the author of this obnoxious innovation was believed to be the republic which had induced Great Britain to acquiesce.

Lately, Italy asked for an economic opening in Asia Minor, into which every Great Power of Europe was penetrating. That the demand was not unreasonable is shown by the fact that it has since been complied with. In view of that contingency, therefore, it would have been well to examine it without bias instead of opposing it with vehemence, for Great Britain is no longer the most puissant state in the Midland Sea and circumstances may one day arise in which she will be in want of an ally there. And Italy is her most natural partner. The circumstances that she is a member of the Triple Alliance is no bar to this prospective co-operation, for the Triple Alliance is a defensive combination. It provides for a certain well-defined eventuality, and outside that sphere, Italy is untrammelled.

The pith of the matter then is that British and French publicists are wont to lay undue stress on Italy's alliance with Germany and Austria-Hungary. That engagement is but a single facet of her activity. There are others more enduring. She is obliged to protect her special interests and is also free to cultivate her special friendships. Paramount among those interests is the maintenance of peace, and chief of those friendships is that with Great Britain and France. Even the Triple Alliance was founded as an association for the prevention of war, and hitherto, it has not drifted into aggression. Italy's influence in that concern is growing and together with it her facilities for upholding the pacific policy with which she has uniformly identified herself. And the more steadily her economic well-being and her political prestige developed, the greater will be the weight which as second member of the alliance she can throw into the scale of peace.

But Italy's role in European politics is a theme which calls for a chapter to itself.

E. J. Dillon

The Contemporary Review, January–June 1913
The World Is Tired of The War

"Prolong a good action," says a Turkish proverb, "and it changes to evil; prolong a bad one and it becomes good." Of this saying, the Balkan War is an apt illustration. Begun as a holy crusade for the liberation of downtrodden Christians in Macedonia, it was continued as a war of conquest and is about to be persisted in as a means of raising money. Even the warmest friends of the Christian belligerents are painfully struck with this discrepancy between start and finish, with the abyss that sunders promise from achievement. The self-sacrificing spirit of the dauntless crusaders, who announced that they did not covet and would not annex a furlong of Turkish territory, fired the imagination and stirred the sympathies of noble-minded people throughout the world. But for the grasping avarice of the thrifty state that now goes ruthlessly on shedding rivers of human blood in the hope of squeezing a milliard francs out of an insolvent adversary, one has only angry disgust. And that is the feeling which Europe entertains today towards those who are primarily responsible for one of the meanest and most cruel struggles on record.

The war, in its present degenerate aspect, reminds me of a story I once heard about a hungry tramp in the country who, though eager for food, was ashamed to beg. He betook himself to a cottage and told the farmer's wife there that he possessed the secret how to cook palatable soup from a stone. The woman's curiosity was whetted. "Let me see you do it," she said. And he began. Dropping *a* clean stone into a saucepan of water, he set the vessel over the fire and waited. As soon as the water was boiling, he stirred it with a spoon, muttering some mysterious words the while, and then he tasted it.

"It is almost ready now," he remarked to his wondering hostess. "A pinch of salt would improve it, perhaps." She brought him the salt. "That is much better," he exclaimed approvingly. "Are you fond of onions? They flavour soup deliciously." She answered that she was, and onions also went into the saucepan. Later on, he induced the simple-minded woman to let him add potatoes, then barley and parsley, and finally bones and meat, with the result that the soup was at last quite good, but nothing less than miraculous. In like manner, the outcome of this war of liberation bids fair to be more lucrative than most campaigns, but the glamour of altruism which at first embellished and ennobled it has faded away. It is becoming a vulgar conflict without an avowable purpose, a mass massacre of brethren as well as of unwilling adversaries, a calamity to several cultural peoples and a disgrace to Europe and humanity.

Petty Tyranny of The Balkan States

The history of the war reveals with peculiar vividness the commanding '*role*' which the little Balkan States have been playing during the past six months and the helplessness of Europe to re-establish peace and restore normal life. At first, the ill-starred people of Macedonia were to have their lot made bearable and, that accomplished, peace would be concluded. That was the status quo phase. Then territorial acquisitions were declared permissible but only up to a certain point. Albania and the coast of the Sea of Marmora were to be inviolable. And now Bulgaria's territorial pretensions extend to the straits, while her money claims are calculated to reduce Turkey to the position of a tributary state, so helpless that she will excite the greed or invite the protection of rival powers. The Ottoman Empire is not being defeated only on the battlefield, it is being pulverised in the Council Chambers. If Bulgaria were to have her way, Turkey would disappear from Asia, as from Europe. And things have already gone so far in this direction that that consummation may occur at any moment, despite the firm will of most of the Great Powers to enable the Turks to eke out a tolerable existence, for Europe is cowed and led by the coalition of exhausted little states, which is now a synonym for Bulgaria. In London, it behoved the delegates to come to terms with Turkey. Every consideration of dignity, national interest, and respect for the interests of the powers prompted them to take this course. They were informed by the ambassadors there that a resumption of hostilities would bring them no further advantages. But they smiled incredulously and told pressmen that they would contrive to harvest in a good deal more at the close of the second campaign. And they spoke with the absolute confidence of men who do not prophesy but say what they know. Europe, in the persons of its diplomatic representatives, adjured them to tarry in London and come to terms with their adversaries. They scouted the notion. Yet during the second campaign, they have made no headway to speak of. Adrianople, Dr Daneff had prophesied, would fall within a week of his departure from London. But the vaticinations of the gifted Bulgarian politician, like those of Jonas, were belied by events. The Servians contributed their quota of auxiliaries to the besiegers, some sixty or seventy thousand men. That was their duty as allies. But they refused to allow them to be sacrificed in an effort to carry the stronghold by storm. "We have not men enough to waste in offering up hecatombs," they explained. So, time had to be entrusted with the task. At Tchataldja, too, the Bulgars have affected nothing. The march on Constantinople is a dream. The Turk has come out of the second campaign immeasurably better than out of the first. At sea, as on land, his exploits command admiration. The renewal of the war was a grievous mistake on the part of the Bulgarians.

Impossible Demands of The Allies

Yet now that peace terms are once more under consideration, that gallant little nation, which gave a splendid example of patriotism to Europe, and an execrable example of diplomatic tactics, has again come forward with claims which the Turks cannot possibly allow. Judging by the articles of the inspired press organs of Sofia and Belgrade, the basis on which the Allies are now willing to discuss peace consists of the following conditions, which will astonish the outsider by their utter ruthlessness: (1) The war is to go on without cessation during the negotiations, and until such time as the treaty is drafted. (2) Turkey is to acquiesce in the boundary line Midia-Rodosto, but may retain the peninsula of Gallipoli; all the territories westwards is to be ceded to the Allies, excepting Albania, the boundaries and organisation of which will be settled at the London Ambassadors' meeting. (3)

Scutari is to be delivered up to Montenegro, and Adrianople to Bulgaria, '*before*' the conclusion of peace. (4) The *Aegean Islands* are to be handed over to Greece. (5) Turkey covenants to pay a war indemnity, the amount of which must be determined before the treaty is signed. (6) Guarantees must be given that the rights of those Christians and subjects of the Balkan States who may reside in Turkey will be respected. This clause amounts to a demand for the privileges enjoyed by subjects of the Great Powers under the capitulations. In the examination and discussion of financial problems arising out of the war, each of the Allies is to be represented by a delegate. And problems enough will be supplied by the clause stipulating that Turkey shall be liable to pay damages for losses she inflicted on the Allies '*before*' the war. New and repellent is the demand that two fortresses which are still heroically holding out, shall be surrendered to an adversary who refuses to respond to this concession by agreeing to an armistice. Then the islands are to be surrendered to the Allies, despite the circumstance that Europe notified its will long ago that they shall be ceded directly to the Great Powers. The Midia-Rodosto boundary line involves a territorial acquisition which would make Bulgaria joint guardian of the straits with Turkey, and as this would modify the existing arrangement, which is guaranteed by treaty; it is also a matter for the Great Powers to adjudicate on. The war indemnity claim is likewise one of the reserved questions.

It is fairly clear, then, that these preliminary conditions will not serve as a base of negotiations, and that the war must drag on indefinitely, until some deus ex machina appears on the scene to stop it, or else Turkey is literally ruined. The circumstance that all Europe is sick of the revolting scenes of blood, and impatient of the pettiness of the leading belligerent state, is of no importance in the eyes of the Balkan diplomatists, for Europe is a negligible quantity. The explanation of this singular attitude would seem to be that the Balkan States rely upon one or more of the Great Powers to espouse their quarrel, if needs be. This confidence may, of course, be misplaced, and all the six powers, without exception, may be resolved to act loyally together. But the Allies have the impression that they can reckon upon a powerful backer among them, and this firm belief emboldens them to snap their fingers at 'united Europe'.

Other motives are also at work. The Allies, for instance, are anxious to gain time, so that Scutari may fall, and Montenegro realise her cherished hopes. This result, which they have for some time been straining every nerve to bring about, would add enormously to the difficulty of the task with which European diplomacy is grappling. And there is some support in recent symptoms for the widespread belief that Scutari is on the point of surrendering. The last onslaught was, military authorities tell me, almost successful. Had the besiegers, who displayed marvellous courage and dash, persisted in their attack for another hour or so, the fortress would certainly have fallen, the Montenegrins would have occupied the town, and the problem how to dislodge them would have become painfully actual. They would not evacuate Scutari at the bidding of Europe. And as Austria will not, cannot, allow the town to be severed from Albania, force would be indispensable to drive away the Montenegrins. Who would undertake the task? Could it be performed without setting the Great Powers by the ears?

The Delimitation of Albania

Scutari has been for a couple of weeks the pivot of the Albanian dispute and the bone of contention between Austria and Russia. After much archaeological talk, the tsar's government let it be divined that unless some new factor is imported into the tangle Scutari might be assigned to Albania, provided, of course, that due compensation is made to the two Slav States. And this bargain was almost struck up when tidings arrived that Scutari might shortly be captured by the besiegers, in which case Montenegro would be desperate if she found that Russia had already, so to say, delivered it over to the enemy. Thereupon, negotiations dragged on, and the question has been left open ever since. Russia's implied assent, therefore, has no binding force if Scutari falls, because it was conditional on the entire Albanian problem being settled among the powers. And this condition has not yet been fulfilled.

Austria-Hungary and Russia, whose points of view are far apart, have not yet agreed on the delimitation of Albania[11] as a whole. The Vienna Foreign Office has been severely blamed by critics at home and abroad for attempting to create this new Balkan State. It can hardly live, they argue, under actual conditions, and in no case will it thrive sufficiently to enable it to discharge the functions which alone would justify the pains taken by Austria to call it into being. And to the dispassionate observer, it certainly looks as though the new organism might be strangled in its infancy. To my own thinking, most of the political conditions dependent upon

---

[11] I am writing on March 15, before the sitting of the ambassadors in London has taken place, at which Russia's decisive answer is expected.

Albania's existence will prove unstable. Whatever terms Turkey may finally be forced or persuaded to acquiesce in, they will not impart finality to the 'equilibrium of forces' in the peninsula. The Balkan Alliance will fall to pieces and other combinations take its place. One Balkan power will expand at the cost of another. At least two groups will be formed which may hold each other in check – for a time. In fine, growth and decay will become so rapid as hardly to be distinguishable from revolutionary processes.

In view of this perspective, the Austro-Hungarian Government is naturally bent on adopting all possible precautions to render its political creation viable. Albania must have territory enough to support a fairly large population. She cannot dispense with the towns and commercial centres which, besides being few, are the principal civilising agencies in the country, and still less can she go without them when they are hers by recognised rights. And that is the case with Scutari, Djakova, Dibra, and several other hotly contested towns and districts. But for peace' sake, Austria has given way to Russia's demand that several such places be abandoned to one or other of the Slav Allies. Dibra, Ipek, Prizrend, Okhrida have one by one been allotted to the Servian peoples. Manifold national and international influences have gradually succeeded in bringing the two rival empires thus near to decisive harmony with the movement of pacific opinion and feeling in Europe. To me, therefore, the optimistic view of the situation taken by British ministers in their public utterances seems fully warranted.

Sir Edward Grey's Proposal

But close together though they stand, Count Berchtold and M. Sazonoff are still divided by a remote little town of some seventeen thousand inhabitants, all but a hundred of whom are Albanians. Djakova is the name of this collection of squalid dwellings for which the politicians of Belgrade clamour on the ground that it belonged to Servia from the fourteenth to the close of the seventeenth century, and that it contains a little convent still regarded as a holy place to which members of the Orthodox Church pilgrimage at times. Austria urges, on the other side, that if any town be Albanian, it is Djakova, in which there are not more than 25 Servian as against 4,100 Albanian houses. It is a cultural centre for Albanian highlanders of the surrounding district, and its loss to Albania would involve permanent damage to the new state. Then again, although Djakova itself is a Moslem town, all the country around is inhabited by Catholics, over whom Austria-Hungary exercises a protectorate. Moreover, the Vienna Cabinet feels that it has already given up much and is unwilling to make further concessions. These are some of the motives which weigh with the statesmen of the Habsburg Monarchy in coming to a decision.

To me, it seems that Austria, having won a series of important diplomatic battles for her protégée, Albania, might well make a supreme effort and abandon Djakova to the Serbs, despite its purely Albanian character, for, after all, the political reconstruction of the Balkans will represent only a transitional state. Before ten years have elapsed, the political map of that part of Europe will have undergone a considerable change. The struggle for national life will begin soon after peace has been re-established, and in the course of it, only the fittest will survive. That is why the interests of the present moment seem to me in this case more pressing than those of the future, which will be safeguarded automatically, as it were, by events which are inevitable and can be foreseen distinctly. Possibly, it was some such train of thought as this which inspired the British Foreign Secretary, to whose resourcefulness and tact in grappling with delicate political problems Europe is deeply beholden, to come forward with a suggestion which seems calculated to feed the wolves while saving the lambs. As the terms of this scheme have never been officially made known, it may suffice to say that it provides for the incorporation of Scutari in Albania, the abandonment of Dibra and its orthodox sanctuary to Servia, and the leaving of the question of Djakova to the decision of an international commission which would visit the district and investigate the claims of the two competing states later on. This proposal contains nothing calculated to wound the dignity or harm the interests of either side and as it offers considerable hope to the Slavs that Djakova may fall to them after all, it is expected that M. Sazonoff will notify his assent. His answer is already overdue by several days, if one may take as one's standard the day on which it was first expected to reach London. As a matter of fact, there is no valid reason why it should come on one day rather than another. But European diplomacy is nervous, therefore impatient, for until Russia's acceptance of this compromise has been given the Great Powers cannot be said to have made any binding arrangement about Albania's frontiers. And if the fortress of Scutari should fall in the meantime, the Montenegrin troops would occupy, fortify, and hold it even though all the Great Powers should exhaust their arsenal of arguments and suasion to dislodge them. And the latter state of things Oriental would be much worse than the first.

Bulgaria And the Race for Scutari

Keenly aware of the valuable prize thus staked on the fate of Scutari, the Slav besiegers are redoubling their efforts to capture it. Montenegro has drawn upon the sister kingdom for reinforcements, and Servia is responding with alacrity. To say with joy, or even readiness, would be to overstrain a point. From what has come to my knowledge, I feel more inclined to say with unwillingness. For the premier, M. Pasitch, a man endowed with a clear political vision, grasps the situation thoroughly. He knows that come what may, Austria-Hungary will not allow the town of Scutari to go to Montenegro. Consequently, all the military operations undertaken with a view to seizing it for King Nicholas, whatever the outcome may be, represent so many men and so much war material wasted. Even the storming of the stronghold would not alter that. In his heart of hearts then, M. Pasitch would, I surmise, say no to his Montenegrin ally if he dared. But he has no choice. In virtue of the military convention subsisting between the two Servian realms, he is bound to furnish the succour demanded. That is why an expedition has been rigged out, and heavy guns, ammunition, camp beds, and all the requisites of war despatched over land '*via*' Elbasan and by water '*via*' Salonica and Durazzo.

It is the Greeks who are conveying their Servian allies to the Albanian coast, and it was while thus engaged that their transport ships were attacked by the Turkish cruiser Hamidieh, five of them damaged, the sixth burned, and all hope of further help from that side shut out for some time.

This attack by the Turkish warship is one of the most brilliant feats of the campaign. It gives one an inkling of what the Turks are capable of accomplishing, on water as on land, if well trained and properly led. In the annals of Turkey's last fight for her European territories, the name of Rauf Pasha will live.

However this may be, I feel that it would be unjust to blame Servia, as so many Austrians have done, for supplying their allies with arms and men. Not if all Europe besought them to deny the request would they be justified in breaking their plighted word. To my mind, it is not a diplomatic theme at all; it is a purely military matter of which the civil government in Belgrade need take no official cognisance. So long as the war lasts the officers in command are alone responsible for conducting it to a successful issue, and no civilian possesses a right to meddle in it. If the Servian Government, like the Italian Cabinet before the war with Turkey, had agreed to abstain from military operations in this or that district or province, such a stipulation would, of course, have to be respected by the commanding generals. But in the case of Scutari, no such limitations can be invoked.

Before leaving this topic about the rights and obligations of the Allies, it may not be amiss to point out a circumstance which has been much and warmly commented on by the separate members of the Balkan Coalition. They complain that Bulgaria is now, and has been ever since the meeting of the Peace Delegates in London, the advocate of a forward policy which renders the conclusion of peace difficult and inflicts huge economic as well as other losses on her partners. It was she who wanted to break off the negotiations weeks before they were actually discontinued. It was she who refused to wait for Turkey's answer and sounded the war trumpet a second time. This she did in spite of the fact that her armies were jaded and unable to undertake any great task single-handed. But her far-seeing statesmen had provided for this contingency. The conventions concluded with the other members of the coalition oblige these to do Bulgaria's bidding, to furnish her with auxiliaries, to help her fight her battles. And the Serbs who had already won everything available that they coveted, were the first to receive the summons. In the matter of keeping their promises, the Serbs are, perhaps, the most scrupulously punctilious of all Balkan peoples. Even in trade, they enjoy an enviable reputation, and I witnessed several instances in which Servian merchants who owed money to Austrian exporters wrote angry letters to them on politics but insisted on paying up long before the bills had fallen due, and in spite of their fixed conviction that war between Servia and Austria was about to be declared.

Well, Servia sent between sixty and seventy thousand troops to Adrianople, whereupon Bulgaria, I am assured, planned the storming of the place at a heavy sacrifice of human life. It is possible that if that scheme had come off, Dr Daneff's prophecy that the fortress would fall within a week of his departure from London would have been wrong only by two or three weeks. But the Servians demurred to this use of their men, the siege was continued, and the former capital of Turkey is still flying the Ottoman flag. So cleverly worded, however, are the military conventions in vigour between Bulgaria and her allies, that not only are they bound thus to come to her aid against Turkey but according to my information they would be also obliged to stand by her were she to quarrel with Roumania.

It is Bulgaria, these people plaintively assert, whose demands now constitute the unique bar to peace. And of these demands, some are set forth, not so much against Turkey as against the powers. The methods, too, but unhappily not also the manners, of the Stamboul bazaar, with its bargaining and beating down of prices, are thus being introduced into diplomacy. The frontier line, from Midia to Rodosto on the Marmora Sea, which Bulgaria persists in demanding, supplies an apt illustration of this kind of haggling. It cannot, of course, be accorded, and Bulgaria is aware of this. If it were agreed to, there would be a tributary state called Turkey but no longer a really independent realm. Constantinople would be cut off from the Dardanelles fortresses, once any foreign military power effected foothold in Rodosto. And what claim has Bulgaria to this asks Turkey. Russia's victorious armies penetrated to San Stefano thirty-five years ago and looked longingly from its heights at the minarets and cupolas of Stamboul. But, for all that, Russia did not suggest that her *protegee's* frontiers should be extended to the Sea of Marmora. In the year 1912–1913, Bulgarian troops, reinforced though they are by well-trained Servian armies, have not pushed near as far as San Stefano, have not even contrived to break through the Tchataldja line. Yet their pretensions exceed those of the triumphant Russians. As I pointed out a couple of months ago, the proposal to leave Gallipoli to Turkey is a mere mockery. Gallipoli, with the Bulgars established in Rodosto, would be an embarrassment, not a help. As a Vienna publicist remarked, it is as though a finger were cut off but left hanging by a bit of the skin.

Bulgaria, those candid Slav critics complain – and the assertion is endorsed by many dispassionate outsiders – is responsible for the bloodshed during this second useless campaign, which she is still perpetuating by asking for terms which Turkey cannot accord nor Europe ratify. The original blunder is already manifest to all. Why is it being aggravated? The political crisis may turn into an economic crisis, from which all Europe and in particular the peoples of Austria-Hungary and the Balkans will suffer terribly. It is of high importance that Europe should intervene and this time efficaciously. Mediation on the lines drawn by Bulgaria is not possible, and people are already asking whether the only workable alternative is not an arbitrament pronounced by the powers and invested with their sanction, irrespective of the whims but mindful of the vital interests of the belligerents.

Sir Edward Grey as Peacemaker

Very curious are the comments on the situation which an ex-Servian Minister publicly makes. I am unable to share the view he takes of the past and the present, but I call attention to it because, if a well-informed Servian official with the knowledge, experience, and patriotism of M. Chedo Miyatovitch holds that Russia is the creator of the Balkan Coalition, then it is not to be wondered at if Austrians believe the story. "The war was practically Russia's work," he writes. "Russia is the real moving and inspiring force behind the Slavonic thrones in the Balkans. From that it is easy to deduce that if Russia wished to stop the war, the war would be stopped to-morrow. Nor is it astonishing that suspicions should be very rife that the renewal of the war was undertaken at a hint from Russia, which found therein the best chances of frustrating the diplomatic success of Austria in Albania." I disagree entirely, with all due deference, with these allegations, and I have reason to know something of what went on before the war and during the negotiations for peace. Russia's attitude throughout was straight, consistent, proper. There was no double-dealing, as there must have been if she had been the initiator of the war and the inspirer of the second campaign. What I do believe – nay, know – is that most of the leaders of the Slav States rely upon unofficial Russia for help, in case of necessity – help which could only be secured by persuading the tsar's government to abandon its standpoint and descend into the arena. But nothing to my knowledge has been said or done by any responsible servant of the crown to confirm this expectation. The delay which has taken place in M. Sazonoff's answer to Sir Edward Grey's proposal was, I believe, referred to by several Vienna press organs as a proof that Russia is taking a hand in the Balkan game against Austria-Hungary and is playing into the hands of the besiegers of Scutari. But, as the Russian proverb has it, 'paper endureth all things'.

Russia has demonstrated in numerous ways the sincerity of her desire to see tranquillity maintained in Europe, and M. Sazonoff's conduct throughout this trying crisis has been that of a chivalrous gentleman, whose word is an adequate exponent of his thought. He has made several important concessions, which materially furthered the cause of European peace, and the delay in coming to a decision on Sir Edward Grey's suggestion is certainly explicable without having recourse to the theory of cunning calculations or diplomatic wiles. He is not the tsar of all the Russia but only the tsar's foreign secretary, and it is not on him alone that it depends to accept or reject the compromise in question.

Meanwhile, I understand that Sir Edward Grey hit upon the most efficacious provisional expedient that could be devised under these difficult circumstances. The problem was how to hinder the Serbs and Montenegrins from persisting in the needless slaughter of human beings before Scutari, until such time as Europe can exert the full measure of its moral pressure by decreeing officially that that town shall be Albanian. And the utmost that could be hoped for was affected; the ambassadors in London unanimously agreed that the delimitation of Albania is a task which the Great Powers alone are qualified to tackle, and that Servia and Montenegro, therefore, are not competent to deal with it. At once ingenious and simple, this finding connotes the nearest approach yet made to a settlement of the most vexatious of all the problems still pressing for a solution. It brings the two rival empires into friendly proximity, removes the most formidable obstacle to a definitive understanding between them, and allows the tidal peace wave, which has been flowing over Europe since 1906, to reach and lave Austria-Hungary and the tsardom.

Austro-Russian Partial Demobilisation

The credit for dovetailing the interests of Austria-Hungary with the peace of Europe belongs wholly to the venerable Emperor Franz Josef, who during the present as well as the last crisis has been the common rallying point of two seemingly divergent tendencies, the furtherance of national aims and the maintenance of the general peace. And now, as then, success has crowned his efforts. His autograph letter to the tsar turned the trembling balance on the side of peace. Its direct consequence was the resolve of both governments to disband the extra troops which had been for some time stationed on either side of the frontier of Galicia. Partial demobilisation is the strongest term one can apply to the measure adopted. Austria-Hungary dismissed to their homes some 33,000 men, while Russia dispensed with the services of 350,900 reservists who had been kept provisionally with the colours. But the measure is only an instalment. The troops which Austria-Hungary has stationed on the southern frontier will not be removed from there until the Albanian problem has been solved and the solution ratified by the powers. But it was not so much the act itself as the spirit which it connoted that was hailed with joyful welcome everywhere. It revived people's drooping faith in the powers of diplomacy, lessened their growing sense of insecurity, and warranted the hope that the powers would draw more closely together for the weal of Europe.

The negotiations that preceded the demobilisation were tedious and not precisely smooth or cordial. Concerning the wording of the official announcement in particular divergences of opinion were wide. The Russian negotiators strove to have a paragraph inserted to the effect that as the result of the exchange of views that had passed between the St Petersburg and the Vienna Cabinets Austria-Hungary harbours no aggressive designs against her southern neighbours. The theses which this declaration presupposes or involves are obvious, and from the Austrian point of view untenable. Discussion, therefore, led to nothing. The proposal was emphatically negatived by Count Berchtold on various grounds which are not devoid of cogency. The policy which Austria-Hungary is pursuing towards the Balkan States, he explained, differs nowise from the policy she followed a month, a year, or ten years ago. Inspired by friendship for those kingdoms, it is bounded by the vital interests and national dignity of the Habsburg Monarchy. Besides, whatever its aims and objects, they do not require the approval, nor are they liable to the examination, of any other state. If a declaration of policy were needed, it was given spontaneously by the Austro-Hungarian Foreign Minister at the delegations in Budapest last November. Finally, he may have objected to the announcement on the ground that it implied Russia's right to protect Servia and in the exercise of that function to call Austria-Hungary to account.

Communiqué and Supplement an Austro-Russian Misunderstanding

After much threshing of logical straw, the two governments agreed upon a form of communiqué which was to appear simultaneously in St Petersburg and Vienna. The obnoxious passage about Austria harbouring no aggressive designs against her neighbours in the South was, of course, eliminated by common accord. But by way of doing everything really feasible to facilitate the difficult task before the Russian Government, which has many and formidable difficulties to grapple with, Austro-Hungarian diplomacy readily undertook to publish a semi-official commentary on the demobilisation in terms which denoted mutual trust, and when the moment came, it duly redeemed its pledge. Surprise and disgust, however, were paramount in Vienna when the telegraph announced that the obnoxious Russian supplement which had been laboriously kept out of the communique had also appeared. It was inserted as a supplement and was open to all the objections enumerated above. A semi-official criticism was at once printed in the Vienna press, and independent Austro-Hungarian organs roundly accused Russia of a breach of faith. "Russia," wrote the Neue Freie Presse, "whether she is willing or reluctant, will be obliged by solicitude for her own dignity and for the good name of her diplomacy to justify herself before the public opinion of Europe for having perpetrated an act which cannot readily be brought into harmony with the honest execution of a stipulated compact."

And yet all the hubbub arose from what, after all, may have been a mere misunderstanding. For on the day when the influential Vienna organ made that stringent comment on the supposed breach of faith, I learned from St Petersburg that the Imperial Russian Government had inserted the supplement objected to only after the Austro-Hungarian Ambassador in that capital had seen and approved it. To the central authorities, however, it had come as a surprise. The incident, one hopes, will have no abiding evil effects. But it has not served to lubricate the international machinery.

Alleged Plan to Extirpate the Albanians

Alleged persecution in Albania, religious and political, will cut much deeper into the relations of the two empires than any such incidents as that of the supplement, because the peoples accused of it are Russia's friends, the Serbs and Montenegrins, against whom the authorities of the Habsburg Monarchy may feel called upon to intervene. The crimes laid to the charge of the two nations are said to have been described with all the requisite particulars by consuls and consular agents and to have been confirmed by local residents worthy of credence. How far this is so, and what worth this evidence may possess when sifted and examined, I am unable to determine. Therefore, I accept no responsibility for the statements, but I vouch for the pain and indignation which belief in their truth has produced in Vienna and other parts of the Dual Monarchy, and likewise for the influence which that feeling may have upon international politics.

The Vienna Cabinet, then, thinks it possesses adequate grounds for believing that the orthodox states, Servia and Montenegro, in their efforts to assimilate the inhabitants of the occupied territory are employing violence against the religions and nationalities in Albania, and that this work of denationalisation and conversion is being carried on with such accompaniments of ferocity that no cultural power in Europe would brook such crimes in its vicinity. It is not only the Albanians who are forced to abjure their religion or to die for their nationality, Slavs who are members of the non-orthodox churches are dealt with in similar fashion. Some of them have been summarily seized, ordered to embrace orthodoxy, and beaten to death, shot, or stabbed for persistent refusal. Apostates are spared, and their ranks are swelling. Moslems have also had to choose between the alternatives of life as renegades, or death as faithful sons of Mohammed. Even among the clergy, there have been victims to this radical method of assimilation. It is employed, however, exclusively in the rural districts. The presence of consuls and other foreigners in town acts as a deterrent, but in remote country parts, the criminals are immune for lack of witnesses to give evidence against them. Everyone is afraid to come forward to tell what he knows. From time to time, however, the general public has had rapid glimpses of sickening deeds of butchery and cruelty which make one wish they were perpetrated by a race different from man; here hundreds of unarmed people huddled together were shot down and put to painful deaths, there women were dishonoured and slain; scores of villages have been razed to the ground. One is told in reply to inquiries that excesses of this kind are inseparable from all wars, and that the crimes in question, so far as they are true, should be laid to the charge of the irregular bands, Komitadjis, and not of the regular troops. Yesterday,[12] the most moderate and the best-informed democratic press organ in Germany[13] received from its correspondent in Uskub the appalling tidings that three hundred Albanians of Luma had just been shot by the Serbs without trial. "In the present case," we read in that paper, "regular Servian troops appear to have organised the blood-bath." And then follows a sensational additional statement which is bound to produce something more than an impression in Europe. I translate it literally:

"We ourselves, at the outset of the war, received from a responsible Servian source this frank announcement: 'We will extirpate the Albanians.' Now that this system of annihilation is being persisted in without modification, despite all European protests, we deem it our duty to reveal the designs of the gentlemen of Belgrade without more ado…In this matter, facts speak more loudly than any confessions could. Since Servian troops crossed the borders last autumn and occupied districts there inhabited by Albanians, one blood-

---

[12] March 15.
[13] Die Frankfurter Zeitung.

bath has followed another in sequence. In isolated cases, the conqueror may have been forced in self-defence to proceed with all martial vigour against an Albanian village from which his troops were perhaps fired on from behind. But to raze hundreds of villages to the ground, to butcher tens of thousands of non-combatants, men, women, and children, these are deeds which no martial law, no precept of self-preservation enjoins..." The writer goes on to say that the Turks having never been able to tame and govern the Albanians, Servia has good reason to believe that she would be still less likely to accomplish this task. "Moreover, what Servia wanted was not new subjects, but new land, and what could be more welcome to her than ownerless land? Thus, from the very start, it was resolved to render Albanian territory so far as it could be conquered ownerless, and from these two motives emanated the order, issued in all secrecy: 'The Albanians are to be extirpated'."

The circumstance that the nations accused of these revolting misdeeds are the liberators whose altruism, valour, and prowess so lately won for them the warm sympathies of the world, adds poignancy to the grief of the friends of the Balkan peoples. For expedients of that primitive kind – assuming that they are really resorted to – argue a radically defective conception of the governance of human beings and warrant Austria in asking whether hundreds of thousands of Albanians should be delivered up to the tender mercies of the people who employ them. The consular narratives were sent to the British and other cabinets, some of which had, it appears, received corroborative testimony from their own representatives. Hope was entertained that they would admonish the responsible governments and thus put a stop to the persecution. The British Government in particular would, it was anticipated, bestir itself in the matter, as representing a sensitive nation, which was stirred to its depths when Bulgarians and Armenians were the sufferers and Turks the criminals. Austria-Hungary felt reluctant to take the matter into her own hands, or to assume the initiative in diplomacy and for reasons which lie fairly near the surface. Action of this kind would be open to misconception.

Austria-Hungary May Intervene in Albania

But the end aimed at has not been attained. Sir Edward Grey, in the House of Commons, emphasised the difficulty in the way of verifying these stories and dwelt on the danger of accepting them as they came from consular offices, for the consul himself has rarely witnessed what he describes. He is at best handing on a narrative of some man or woman in whose veracity he has confidence and on such hearsay evidence it would be unwise to take action calculated to unleash popular passion. That was the ground occupied by the British Government, which is in no hurry, seeing that the matter is not pressing. But Austria-Hungary cannot afford to treat the phenomenon thus academically. The problem must be dealt with. Accordingly, a protest has now been formally lodged, and if this procedure also proves unavailing, and fail to do away with the scandal, the Vienna Cabinet will, I understand, test the efficacy of other and less gentle methods. Public feeling in both halves of the monarchy is aroused against the authors of these atrocities, and public opinion is clamouring that a speedy end should be put to them.

And the deepest spirit of the monarchy prompts the cabinet to show itself responsive to the blaze of anger which thus fires the spokesmen of the nation. Nobody cares whether there is any or no connection between the political issues before the powers and these manifestations of the human beast. Whether the victims of this infamous method are Albanians or Slavs, Christians or Moslems, is also immaterial. The approach to cordiality in the intercourse between the Russian and Austro-Hungarian Governments does not lessen the guilt of the persecutors, nor soften the wrath of their neighbours. The grievance stands alone and will be dealt with on its merits by the powers, if they are prompt enough, otherwise, by Austria-Hungary herself. And if the government should resort to intervention, it will not even invoke the right claimed and exercised for generations by the Austrian Emperors to protect the Catholics of Albania. Yet the correlate of this right is an obligation which no conceivable contingency could well render more peremptory or more pressing than the persecution now complained of.

The motive force of the intervention which will infallibly take place, unless these sanguinary practices are speedily abandoned, is intelligible without any reference to political problems. The Emperor Franz Josef will vindicate rudimentary humanity in South-Eastern Europe and emancipate the people of the provinces in question from a yoke which, if these tales are true, is worse than that from which the Allies have now rescued their countrymen.

That intervention will be resorted to, if the appeal to the powers prove unavailing, is a foregone conclusion. It is for the purpose of making this alternative clear enough to be grasped by all whom it may concern that I have touched upon the repellent topic. *As* for the allegations themselves, I repeat that I am unable to confirm or question them.

One All-Important Outcome of The Balkan War

Amid the saturnalia of suddenly liberated energies, political, racial, and social, which the downfall of Turkey has inaugurated, it is not easy to see through and beyond the ephemeral activity of each of the heterogeneous factors, nor to discern or foretell the issue of the process. The quick transitions and bewildering phases of action and reaction, the flux and reflux of conflicting aims and contending principles, render it difficult to keep one's gaze fixed on the flow of the main current of history. And yet most of the phenomena which thus perplex us have a common root: the attitude of the Balkan States, and the determined efforts of Russia to play the part of guardian to them; the creation of an independent Albania; the dragging on of a purposeless war; the vast increase, of the German Army, already the most formidable on the globe and the corresponding strengthening of all the armies and navies, with the revival of the military spirit in France, are all consequences of the same phenomenon. Below the surface of the apparent anarchy of international politics are the usual forces, the interplay of which keeps humanity progressing, and by dint of pulling down and building up evolves new types of civilisation. The new order clashes with the old, pioneers become obstructors, temporary losses end in permanent gains, and the human race moves fitfully forward.

A racial struggle, it seems to me, lies at the root not only of the crisis produced by the defeat of Turkey but of all the complexities of the European situation. The fibres of race, so to say, are entwined with the heartstrings of politicians. The Balkan campaign has raised domestic problems there into another sphere and transformed the strife of petty political interests into a titanic struggle of races, of which we now witness but the first faint stirrings. On the issue of the coming Slavo-Teutonic might contest hangs the future of Europe.

And yet no pressing danger threatens the peoples of the continent. Between Russia and Germany, official relations are friendly. In their respective aims and policies, there is nothing incompatible; there are no differences that cannot be readily smoothed down with average good-will. But the so-called equilibrium of military forces has been visibly upset to the detriment of the Triple Alliance, and the sight of the unexpected change may, it is thought, operate as a stimulus to the energy, a reviver of the traditional aims and a decisive factor in swaying the Near-Eastern policy of Russia. Slavdom has scored a grandiose and abiding success. It is moving to the Adriatic and will sweep away the Turk. And the Triple Alliance has undergone a corresponding reverse. As yet both loss and gain are potential, as when the holder of securities learns that his shares have fallen twenty points. If he can afford to keep them until prices recover, all is well. But if it is certain that prices cannot ever improve but may fall still further, his loss is as inevitable as though he had realised it. Well, that, it is held in Germany, is the position of the Triple Alliance today, and still more is it the position of the German peoples, between whom and the Slavs a struggle for life must one day be fought out.

Accordingly, in Austria's calculations for the future of the peninsula, the Balkan states are divided into two groups, say,

Bulgaria, Roumania, and Albania on the one side, and Servia, Greece, and Montenegro on the other. As the moral fibre of the Bulgarians is vigorous, and their political and military equipment considerable, Austria-Hungary's position in the new order of things would be no whit less satisfactory than it was in the old. In many ways, indeed, it would be more advantageous. But a searching analysis of the conditions that prevail in the Balkans will show how problematic this reckoning is. Roumania's policy, which has heretofore been easily directed by the king, will undergo uao modification, so long as the present monarch continues to reign. But afterwards? Again, it is a mark of an over-sanguine mind to assume that, as Bulgaria's attitude was for many years antagonistic to Russia and distinctly friendly to Austria-Hungary, therefore it must be Slavophobe in the future. Bulgaria has never been Austrophile or Russophile. In everything she did and eschewed in the past, she consulted her own interests and none other. And her policy of the future will be inspired by the same considerations. Consequently, the only certain result of the Balkan War is an enormous uplifting of the Slav race and a corresponding growth of its military resources in the South and in the North.

Heretofore, the Triple Alliance could lean on Turkey in the South-East, inasmuch as the Ottoman Army, with its splendid material and glorious traditions could hold the Slav states of the Balkans in check, and to some extent Russia as well. A large contingent of the land defences of the Slav nations would thus be immobilised in the vicinity of the Turkish frontiers. And that immobilisation would allow Austria-Hungary to move her armies whithersoever she listed. Such was the state of affairs before the war broke out.

Today, all that is changed. The Turks have virtually departed from Europe, and whether they will long remain as rulers in Asia is very dubious. But, in any case, the land forces of Austria-Hungary will to a large extent be absorbed in case of war by Servia and by Servia's allies and will not be available for use at any other front, say, in supporting Germany. Consequently, to that extent at least, the Triple Alliance has been weakened, and the increase of Germany's army is explained. Politicians may welcome or deplore the unexpected collapse of the once mighty empire, which bade fair a few centuries ago to spread to Central and Western Europe, but it behoves the statesman to provide for what is coming and to have everything in readiness to readjust his methods to the new set of conditions the moment they have come into being. And that is precisely what the German Government is doing.

Germany's Call to Arms and Alms

So long as we keep clearly in view the vast changes which, potential ever since the Treaty of Berlin, have become real and palpable only after the victories scored by the Balkan Coalition, we shall recognise, I do not say the justification but the explanation of the mighty efforts, military, financial, and moral, which the German nation is now putting forth. For South-Eastern Europe is becoming the arena of Slav and Teutonic forces, which must one day clash and determine their respective places in Europe by an appeal to arms. Of this necessity, the Russians, or say rather a certain section of that people, would seem to have an instinctive, a semi-conscious inkling. This new factor, long in evidence as a likely, contingency, has today been introduced into the sphere of

European politics, where in coming years it will play a predominant part. The Slav, as well as the Teuton, is predestined to contribute elements peculiarly his own to the work of cultural progress. But the race differences between the two, which display themselves in the objects directly pursued and in the means employed to attain them, are so incompatible that before the races can combine, they will produce a ferment.

Meanwhile, Germany is offering an example of rare foresight or folly in her military preparations and of civic virtue in pecuniary sacrifices by which they are to be made feasible. The contingent of recruits is to be increased by 84,000 men yearly, an addition which will raise the peace strength of the army by about 170,000 so that it will number 828,000 in future, instead of 660,000 as hitherto. The cost of this measure, together with its corollaries, will lay upon the taxpayers of the Fatherland an annual impost of ten million pounds and a bulk sum of a thousand million marks (fifty million pounds). When we remember that in the year 1912 the outlay on Germany's national defences on land and water amounted to the goodly total of 1,410,000,000 marks (£70,500,000), we begin to realise the grim earnest of the people, of whom we have been taught to believe that they are rich in children but poor in money. As a matter of fact, the average individual Briton may be better off than the average German or Frenchman, but there is reason to believe that between the Frenchman and the German there is no noteworthy difference in this regard.

France, who is resolved not to lag behind in this race for military superiority, intends to reintroduce the three years' military service – a terrible tax on the wealth-creating elements of the country – which will give her an increase of 160,000 men in peace. At present, the peace strength of the French Army is – if we exclude colonial troops – 534,000, and after the new law has received force, it will number 750,000. Russia, whose wealth in men is inexhaustible, is minded to raise her peace effective to 1,800,000 men, of whom Europe will possess 1,350,000. It is France who has to make the most strenuous exertions to keep abreast of her rival, owing to her relative dearth of males. With a population of less than fifty million, she will dispose of 750,000 troops in time of peace, whereas Austria-Hungary, with fifty-two million, will be contented with 450,000. In Germany, there is said to be a strong feeling against the drastic methods by which the thousand million marks are to be raised. It is at bottom a war-tax in peace time. It will fall heavily on retired merchants, widows, and invalids, who possess a moderate fortune, on the interest of which they eke out a modest existence. The idea is said to have originated in the fertile brain of the Kaiser himself. It may well be. Brilliant and practical it undoubtedly is but Bismarck, were he living, would probably have criticised it on the ground of its running counter to the law of the economy of forces. Keep your sledge-hammer for great masses of metal; do not use it to kill flies. In wartime, the milliard tax would have been a genial scheme; to employ it in peace is to be guilty of wanton waste.

Among the voices, few and weak, which have been lifted up against the tax and the military measure that provoked it, one may be quoted for its directness. *"Militarism,"* writes a German paper, "is eating us up. With dread the patriot asks: Whither will all that lead us? *At present five years' peace costs us* as much as, or even more than, a lost campaign would have cost us yesterday."[14]

E. J. Dillon

---

[14] Der Bayrische Kurier.

The Contemporary Review, June 1914

Albania To Be or Not to Be?

It is hardly an exaggeration to affirm that despite or, perhaps, in consequence of the efforts of European diplomacy the Balkan tangle has become more bewildering than ever before. The latter state, which was to have been a sort of miniature millennium, is considerably worse than the former, at least in its international aspect. For the Conference of London, like the Congress of Berlin, introduced into its peace work the germs of strife unending. Desirous of scoring a temporary political victory, this power or that insisted on a delimitation of peoples and territory in which the populations most nearly interested are resolved not to acquiesce, and as they have the will and the power to indulge in perpetual strife, it is greatly to be feared that respect for the decision of Europe will not check them. And what is even more to the point, the ends for which these unnatural combinations were devised will not be achieved. On the contrary. And some of the states which benefited by this distribution of the spoil will find in the long run that the blessing is a curse in disguise, for they have swallowed more than they can assimilate.

Of Greece, this is hardly true. She can absorb without difficulty the ethnic and territorial morsels which have been allotted to her. But there are good grounds for the contention that Servia will find her task of assimilation more than she can manage with comfort. And from the Servian and Slav point of view, this is a consummation to be regretted. What it means is that Servia will be forced by the never-ending troubles fomented by her new subjects to expend so much money and national vitality in absorbing them, that she will be too weak to further her other and more momentous interests, and may, after a few years of enfeebling exertions, find herself at the mercy of any Great Power that likes to 'protect' and advise her. That, it seems to me, is one of the consequences of the work of the London Conference. The members of that assembly were all eminently well-intentioned, and they did the best they could for the peace of Europe according to their lights and their means. Sir Edward Grey, in particular, deservedly won golden opinions for the moderating influence which he exerted at a moment when political passion ran high and calm reasoning was at a discount. He succeeded in achieving the most satisfactory result attainable. But unhappily, the best attainable turns out to be a poor safeguard of peace and order in the Balkans.

The creation of Albania was a by-product of the process of redistribution, and it was treated as such, Albanian towns and villages being bestowed on states which may soon discover that they are hornets' nests and not the beehives which they fancied them. The allotment of market towns to Servia and Montenegro, for instance, which are absolutely necessary to the populations of the adjoining highland districts still belonging to Albania, was, I venture to think, one of the most disastrous mistakes committed by the conference, for no community can sit still and see its daily bread taken away in order to gratify the whim of a neighbour. The Albanian community is no exception to the rule, and there is reason to fear that prolonged frontier troubles will be one of the effects of this ill-judged measure.

I write these lines at Tirana in Albania. I have already discussed the position and outlook of this ill-starred country with every personage of note in Durazzo, Scutari, and other places, and the conclusions to which I am forced are not calculated to warrant optimism. I feel convinced that this newly created state possesses all the essential conditions of a viable political community. The people are intelligent, honest, willing to work, sober, and endowed with remarkable staying powers. True, the impress of centuries of Turkish misrule is visible in the lack of roads, bridges, telegraphs, schools, in the administration of justice, and other necessaries of a well-ordered community. But the population is, on the whole, pacific and docile and emulated by a burning desire to lend a hand in building up the new state. I have met Albanian physicians and diplomatists who spontaneously sacrificed the emoluments of lucrative callings and have come to Durazzo in order to give their fellow citizens the benefit of their culture and experience. Turkhan Pasha abandoned an embassy. M. Nogga gave up diplomacy and, suppressing his ambitions, offered his valuable services to the new sovereign. Others made similar sacrifices. The resulting outlook was correspondingly cheerful. The minister of finances, M. Nogga, whose task is superlatively thankless, will be able in less than four years to balance revenue and outlay without a deficit; the Department of Public Instruction is ready with a practical programme of education, which seems admirably adapted to the needs of the people. The minister of public works has drawn up a list of measures by which the indispensable wants of the country will be provided for. The desirability of disarming the population has been taken into consideration, and the ways and means of carrying it out without provoking troubles have been devised and approved. In a word, everything which Europe could reasonably expect from the Albanians themselves is become feasible, and all that is now needed is the signal to set the machinery in movement and begin to work. But the signal unhappily cannot be given, and stagnation is the result.

For Albania is confronted in the South with a rebellion which differs little from a war. The Epirotes are up in arms against her and demand, as the price of their submission, that the country around Koritza and Argyrocastro be declared two provinces with autonomous administration and a centrifugal tendency which may culminate in separation. The Albanian Government refuses to accept the theory that this is a rebellion. It holds that the population is submissive enough and desires only to be left in peace, but that it is terrorised by bands, reinforced by Christian troops, who deserted from the Turkish army during the war, and by a body of Cretans who embarked openly at Corfu and are now spreading terror through the land. Blood is flowing copiously. Villages are being burned. Thousands of inoffensive men, women, and children are being turned adrift houseless, penniless, helpless. Between sixty and seventy thousand refugees from there, the province of Dibra and the Montenegrin frontier, are quartered upon Albania, whose government has to spend in keeping them from starvation a portion of the four hundred thousand sterling which were given as an advance on a future loan. The infant state is unable to defend its people for lack of officers, heavy guns, and money. When Essad Pasha rigged out an expedition to make a stand against the Epirotes, and asked for the necessary funds to supply them with food and ammunition, the Commission of International Control vetoed the expenditure on the ground that the soldiers, not being officered by trained men, constituted a body of irregulars who might commit excesses and could not be paid with the money of the powers. In a word, the plight of those to whom the task of regenerating the country has been confided, is pitiable.

The creation of Albania was the deliberate act of the Great Powers. It implied at the very least the resolve of those powers to see that the conditions of national existence were tolerable and that the Albanian people would have a reasonable opportunity of showing their capacity for self-government and cultural development. But the actual conditions render this task impossible. Instead of addressing themselves to the work of peaceful consolidation, the Albanian Ministers are forced to equip a military expedition and to waste their slender resources on an unnecessary and unfruitful war. And even this they have to do without sufficient money, any officers, or artillery! If, under the circumstances, the experiment proves a failure, as it may well do, Europe will have itself to blame for the consequences which may reach further and cut deeper than people at present realise. Albania was born under an unlucky star. Its territory was whittled away, and its population reduced to 900,000. And now, it is being further lacerated and its people thinned and impoverished by neighbours in the Northwest and the South.

For the moment, hostilities between the Epirotes and the Albanians have been suspended in virtue of an armistice, and negotiations are proceeding between the chief of the insurgents, Zographos, and the Commission of International Control. The Albanian Government, which I am able to say is wisely guided by the young king, '*so far as his influence extends*', has offered a number of privileges to the Greek element of Epirus. M. Zographos holds out for more, and if he insists, he can probably obtain autonomy. But this result would stimulate others to make similar demands, and in a few months, the country would be rent asunder. Meanwhile, Europe looks on attentively but makes no move. The resulting situation is tragi-comical. It warrants the biting remark of a diplomatist of my acquaintance, who said: "Europe is always agreed as to the necessity of agreeing but never as to the necessity of acting."

E. J. Dillon

The Contemporary Review, July 1914

Albania's Tribulations And Colonel Phillips

Albania emerged from the diplomatic operating-room mutilated and enfeebled. Not only were important districts severed by the powers and annexed by her neighbours but even the narrow boundaries finally set by Europe have not been respected. And the new state, before it could be consolidated, before it had received a regular government, was confronted with a rebellion in the South and with the imminent danger of an invasion in the North, and was destitute of a regular army and financial resources to meet the emergency. The northern peril, which was the more formidable of the two, was averted by the English Colonel Phillips, in his twofold capacity as governor of Scutari and commander of the international troops there. This officer possesses the confidence of the Mohammedan as well as the Catholic elements of the population and wields a degree of authority over both, which neither his position nor his real power could have conferred upon him. They feel drawn towards him by his straightforward methods, which take account of their habits of thought and modes of action, and by his sense of justice, which they appreciate even when it brings them disappointment. Hence, he can hold them back by a word and attune them to patience by touching the right chord and generally get the better of their impulses and render them amenable to reason. In this way, he hindered them from retaliating on the Slavs, whose impulsive warriors had crossed the borders, taken possession of certain contested strips of land, and generally provoked the Albanians to fight.

Those stretches of contentious land are the creation of the International Boundary Commission. In fixing the limits between Albania and its Slav neighbour, the delegates of Great Britain, Germany, Austria, and Italy drew one line, giving to Albania what, to their thinking, belongs of right to it, while the Russian and French, assigning a number of Albanian villages to Montenegro, proposed another line. And as unanimity is required before the boundary can be definitely fixed, the territory between the two provisional frontiers is for the time being a sort of Tom Tiddler's land. But only the Montenegrins are wont to go there, and they shoot any Albanian who ventures to do likewise. Further, the official representatives of King Nicholas collect taxes, seize arms, and rule the inhabitants without let or hindrance. This state of things is full of perils. Those Albanians, who are under Colonel Phillips's jurisdiction and also those who are beyond it, are naturally eager to learn which are the frontiers of the country. But the Boundary Commission cannot agree on the subject. Altogether the English Governor has a difficult task to perform, and the means at his disposal are absurdly inadequate, he is expected to maintain order not merely in the ten-kilometre circuit, which is particularly under his care, but also over a large stretch of country extending southwards to the River Matya [Mat], and for this purpose, he disposes of just sixty gendarmes and insufficient funds. Nor is he fully master in his own district. Numerous contentious matters have to be referred to the International Commission of Control, and this estimable body, presumably absorbed by graver matters, leaves most of these inquiries unanswered. Some weeks ago, the Albanian authorities decided in the interests of their country to extend Colonel Phillips's jurisdiction over all Northern Albania. But this beneficent scheme was promptly negatived by one of the Great Powers – one of Albania's protectors. This is in perfect harmony with all arrangements in that ill-starred country, which is symbolised by ruined huts, abortive plans, and unfulfilled intentions.

The Fortnightly Review, July 1 1914
The Albanian Tangle

Albania is a problem of intense political interest flavoured by a spice of political danger. It was set before Europe by way of warding off a greater and more perilous problem which would, however, have confronted only two allies, who in this matter are rivals – Italy and Austria-Hungary. As members of the Triple Alliance, these two states are bent on upholding the present equilibrium on the Adriatic, and as rivals, each one grudges the other any acquisition of territory or increase of influence there. In particular, the Albanian harbour of Valona is strategically of such vast importance to an Adriatic State that neither of these two can allow the other to take possession of it, come what may. For this reason alone, therefore, had there been none other, the creation of the new realm of Albania was a political necessity for Italy and Austria. But it was also an act of justice towards one of the oldest and hardiest races of the continent and was construed as such by Europe. For it is idle to deny the existence of an Albanian race, and it would have been folly to ignore it. Under the crushing weight of Turkey, the Albanians alone, of all the Christian peoples of the Balkans, kept their national physiognomy and their racial consciousness intact. Religion itself – at all times an irresistible solvent of ethnical cement in the Turkish Empire – was powerless to sap the foundation of Albanian nationality. And the Turk grasped this characteristic trait and utilised it to the utmost, humouring the idiosyncrasies of the Arnauts and employing them against the turbulent elements, Christian and Moslem, of the Ottoman Empire. It was in order to have this redoubtable force always at its beck and call that the Porte systematically encouraged the simple-minded highlanders to hold aloof from their neighbours, to preserve their secular customs, to maintain their ancient feudal order, and to observe their clumsy substitutes for law.

The establishment of an Albanian State was therefore the direct and necessary outcome of the sudden shifting of the equilibrium in South-Eastern Europe. And as the Albanians themselves were largely answerable for this displacement, one may truly affirm that they too contributed materially to their own renascence. It was in the name of their nationality that they resisted stubbornly under conditions of disheartening inferiority the forces of the Ottoman Empire. Nationality is the cement which kept the Albanians intact under Rome, Byzance, the Norman Conquest, the Venetian domination, and Ottoman misrule. But only the Albanians, among all the other Christian peoples of the East nationality, when tested, proved unavailing to achieve this result. Religion was the balm which saved their dead political bodies from corruption under the Osmanli. Those among them who remained true to their creed might suffer hardship or death for their fidelity, but at any rate, the survivors were not absorbed by the Turk, whereas all the weak-kneed who embraced Islam were at once bereft of their nationality, like the Vlachs, the

Pommaks, the Bosniaks, and others. On the contrary, an Albanian who changed his faith never forfeited his nationality as a consequence. Whether he became Orthodox or Moslem, or remained Catholic, he was always an Albanian and was treated as such by his kindred. Nowhere in the Balkans has nationality been so deep-rooted as among the people of the Shkipetar race.

This characteristic, which has never been properly analysed or even understood in Europe, was utilised by Abdul Hamid, who, when he found his Christian subjects slipping from his grasp under the championship of the European Powers, endeavoured to colonise the territories still remaining to him by the two highland races which he could use as docile instruments in peace time as in war: the Kurds in Asia Minor and the Albanians in the Balkans. In normal years, he sent them to colonise Christian districts and in wartime to drive out the obnoxious inhabitants. And for the purpose of preserving his faithful Albanians in their pristine ignorance of the new spirit which was blowing from the West over all the peoples of Eastern Europe, and rendering them impatient of misrule, he isolated the people, closed native schools, penalised the use of the Latin alphabet, forbade the printing of Albanian books, punished every attempt at organisation, discouraged the development of the material resources of the country, and prohibited the construction of roads and the building of bridges[15].

But the Young Turks undid his work and blundered in this as in so many other matters of imperial import. At first, they

---

[15] One of the few writers who appears to have gauged rightly the trend of Abdul Hamid's Albanian policy is Louis Jaray, *Questions Diplomatiques et Coloniales*, No. 411.

encouraged and then proscribed liberal ideas, and they ended by a mad attempt to root out the one ineradicable trait of the Albanian race – its national consciousness. The results are recorded by history.

For the right of opening Albanian schools and having their children taught in their mother tongue and writing their language with suitable letters, the Albanians sacrificed their substance and their lives. And it was largely the effort to overcome this stout resistance that sapped the strength of the Turks and fatally handicapped them in the campaign against the Balkan League. It is seriously therefore to over-rate the part played by political expediency in the formation of the new community to assert that the scheme was devised solely by Austria and Italy for their own behalf. The statesmen of Vienna and Rome set the hallmark of international diplomacy upon a combination which a host of other circumstances rendered indispensable and pressing. Had this necessity been clearly perceived and rightly gauged at the outset, there would have been fewer sneers at the wild experiment and less scepticism when baffling obstacles were first encountered.

What the European public is now eager to learn – if there be anyone able to answer the query – is whether the new state can live, thrive, and discharge the useful functions which the powers have assigned to it, or whether the intricate and multitudinous growths which now seemingly overspread the land will choke off all fruitful endeavour and call for a solution more radical and less ephemeral than fitful direction and temporary military occupation. The latter assumption has hardened to conviction in the minds of many since the recent outbreak of troubles in the centre of Albania and the flight of the Royal Family. But it is still too soon to instance these deplorable occurrences as proofs that the state-building experiment is an egregious failure. It would be more correct to include those untoward events – considered apart – among the ills from which no inchoate state – and least, of all one born under such adverse circumstances as Albania – is ever immune. Instead of launching out into prophecies which tomorrow's ups and downs may belie, it will be more helpful to dwell on the essential conditions of Albania's existence, the narrow boundaries set to opportunity, the lack of everything needed for consolidation, and the disturbing interplay of foreign influences with the national character, and to leave the reader to shape his own forecast.

Albania then was born with the taint of original sin – which will of necessity tarnish all her future activity. A considerable part of her territory and a large section of her population were severed from the trunk, so to say, and grafted on Montenegro and Servia.

This was the handiwork of Europe, impelled by motives alien to the welfare of the new nation. It was a repetition of the sinister course taken by the powers at the Congress of Berlin, and one may well fear that it will be followed by like mischievous consequences. Then the provinces severed from Turkey were so distributed that each of the little states which received a part received together with it the bitter hatred of one of its neighbours in whose territory that part ought in fairness to have been incorporated. At the London and Bucharest Conferences, a similar course was struck out. Instead of rigging out the new state with the essential territorial conditions of vitality, and keeping together all the compact Albanian population, several villages, towns, and districts were lopped off and then spliced together with the

Slavs whom they hate and by whom they are hated. And this ethnical vivisection was not the result of a mistake; it was affected with deliberation and foreknowledge of the inevitable results.

One motive for this unnatural division was Austria's resolve to deprive Servia of an outlet to the Adriatic and to use Albania as a bar between her and that waterway. The expediency of this attitude towards Servia, I am not now concerned to discuss, but what I feel, and feel strongly, is that the work of fashioning Albania into an independent state ought to have been undertaken on its own merits and under the most favourable circumstances possible. Thus, there should have been no hampering conditions, no need of mutilating the new state in order to compensate Servia for her exclusion from the Adriatic. As it happened, however, Austria was worsted in a series of wearisome wordy battles and forced to give up one after another Albanian villages, towns, and districts which have since been incorporated in Montenegro and Servia. Albania thus became a mere torso which may prove unable to stand alone in the midst of vastly superior organisations, military and political, nearly all of them eager for her partition. Servia denies Albania's right to exist and is ready when opportunity serves to draw the practical corollary from this negation. Montenegro and Servia are destined in the near future to unite and form one Slav kingdom hostile to the new realm, which needs all its sons to withstand the onslaught that will one day be made against it. Meanwhile, thousands of these hardy mountaineers, together with their wives and children, have been driven out of their homes by their new masters and are on their way to Anatolia, where some provision is being made for their reception by the Turkish Government. I have met steamers crowded with them.

Under such conditions, there is little hope that peace will be of long duration in the Balkans. One of the sources of trouble there which will make itself felt before all others is a direct consequence of that unfair partition which gives to the Slavs the market towns of which the Albanian peasants have absolute need – for they cannot dispense with them and live. Hence, a fierce struggle for life is certain to break out. The Dibra Valley, for example, is surrounded by lofty mountains, the inhabitants of which have no place to buy or sell except the city. They are isolated by distance and by geographical situation from every other market, especially in winter. Yet the mountains are now part of Albania, while the valley and city, which are economically indispensable to the mountaineers, have been annexed by Servia. It is not difficult to foresee the results of this artificial arrangement. As a matter of fact, they were foreseen and foretold by Baron von Giesel and myself during the London Conference, and neither of us could then believe that the irrational combination would be assented to by any body of men free to affect a fair partition on its own merits. But the ambassadors in London were not thus free. They had to allow for considerations of an extrinsic order and were well aware that the division of the land which they imposed upon the discontented states would lay upon coming generations, and perhaps on the present one, crushing burdens in strife and bloodshed. In annexing archi-Albanian districts, Servia and Montenegro have donned each a Nessus' shirt, while Albania by incorporating the Greeks of Epirus has been forced to do the same.

It was this contentious matter of Epirus which stirred up the anger of the Greeks and confronted the Albanian Government with its first mishaps. The district to be annexed was inhabited by people who, whatever their real origin, deemed themselves Greeks, spoke the Greek tongue, and resented being handed over to the rulers of a state so much less cultured than themselves. Their representative, an earnest patriot, M. Vamvakas, journeyed through Europe to lay the desire of his countrymen, who asked for annexation to Greece, or at least autonomous government, before the statesmen of Europe. In vain. Europe's decision had already fallen, and against it, there was no diplomatic appeal. But aware of the weakness of Europe to enforce its own decrees when the interests of one of the Great Powers are not involved, the people of Epirus took the law into their own hands as they had threatened, raised the standard of rebellion, constituted a provisional government under M. Zographos, and captured villages and towns which the regular forces of the Hellenic Government had vacated. Whether and to what extent they were reinforced by officers and privates of the regular army, is a secondary point which I am not concerned to discuss. The pith of the matter is that Albania, receiving no help from without, was left by Europe to assert and uphold its rights over the territory as best it could. And it was left without the means.

The ensuing effort of the Albanian Government to put down the rebellion involved the country in unmixed evils. The cabinet resolved to equip an expedition against the Epirotes and requested the International Commission of Control to authorise the requisite expenditure. This the commissioners refused to do on the ground that the contingent thus formed would consist of untrained soldiers without competent officers, and that deplorable excesses on the part of both might reasonably be apprehended. Against this objection, it was urged that the only alternative to a native army was the despatch of European forces for the purpose of giving effect to Europe's decision, and that a definite and speedy choice of one of these courses seemed a necessary corollary of Europe's attitude and Albania's plight. As the latter had been rejected, the former became imperative. The ministers added that they would themselves guarantee that no atrocities would be allowed to embitter the struggle. But Europe's representatives were inexorable.

Essad Pasha, as war minister and home secretary, was charged by his sovereign with the work of raising recruits in Central Albania for this expedition. He addressed himself to the patriotism of the people, but his appeal fell on deaf ears. The villages that had once acknowledged his sway, like Shiak, Tirana, Kavaya, forbade their fighting men to volunteer for a Christian prince and his renegade Mussulman Minister who was responsible for bringing over that prince. Thereupon, the work of enlistment came to a standstill. I was with Essad at the moment when the telegram announcing this decision was handed to him, and I noted with curiosity the effect it had. He boiled with rage, hurled ejaculatory phrases at the rebels, and without losing a moment dashed off to Shiak and Tirana to call them to account. Here his success was only partial. At first, they ventured to reproach, revile, and assail him, but he daunted them by his presence and his intrepidity. The Albanians know a strong man when they see him. The dispositions which Essad subsequently took for taming the insubordinate villagers and despatching the troops southwards were avidly seized upon by his personal enemies, construed as parts of a plot to kill the king, overthrow the government, and hand over Albania to the Young Turks. The discovery of the alleged conspiracy was kept secret, Essad, who was war minister, home secretary, and acting vizier in one, was vigilantly watched, and when the propitious hour had struck, he became a target for balls and bullets and was finally shipped from Albania into exile.

That high-handed act, for which as yet no explanation or excuse has been offered, was followed by a series of risings in the country, which one party ascribes to Essad's perfidious machinations and the other to the treacherous attack on the trusty and loyal servant of the king. So far as I can judge, both explanations are unfounded.

But frontier troubles were by no means exhausted by the Epirote rising in the South. The Serbs and Montenegrins were hardly less aggressive than the Epirotes. The subjection of the Hoti and Gruda clan was accompanied by the flight of thousands of necessitous tribesmen into Scutari, whose arrival thrust the inhabitants of that city into dismay. The British Governor, Colonel Phillips, on taking over the governorship, had been assured by his predecessors, the admirals, that everything was in order, that the refugees would not exceed a few hundred, and that ample provision had been made for their reception and keep. Events belied this optimistic forecast. Nineteen thousand fugitives swept down the hills one day and strained the resourcefulness of the governor to the utmost. He drove most of them back and made provision for nearly two thousand, despite the circumstances that there were no funds available for them.

At the same time, the International Boundary Commission became a fruitful, if unwitting, source of strife and bloodshed. In drawing the line of demarcation between Montenegro and Albania, the commissioners were not at one. The British, German, Austrian, and Italian representatives were for according certain hamlets and strips of territory, which they deemed Albanian, to the government of Durazzo, whereas the French and the Russian representatives held that they should be assigned to the Slav State. And as unanimity of votes was necessary for a definitive settlement, the two lines were drawn provisionally. Within these lines, the Montenegrins are wont to foregather and shoot any Albanian who dare to trespass on them, and the British Governor of Scutari was helpless to prohibit the encroachment or punish the murderers. Colonel Phillips also received messages announcing that if a single Montenegrin were shot, the Cettinje Government would pour its troops into Albania forthwith.

Against those disorders, there was no remedy, and the fact that peace and order have been maintained in the city of Scutari and over a large district to the North and North-East, reaching to the River Matya [Mat], despite those difficulties and other artificial obstacles, constitutes an achievement of which Colonel Phillips and his country have reason to be proud.

From these perturbations of foreign origin, even the centre of Albania is not immune. Young Turkish emissaries, professional and amateur, wandered into the district, stirred up the misery – stricken villagers against their Christian ruler and his government from whom they expected so much and received nothing, decided Essad Pasha as a traitor and a renegade who was making common cause with the giaour and the foreigner, and in this way spread disaffection among the benighted peasants. Djemal Bey, who is a major of the Ottoman General Staff, Arif Hikmet, an ex-journalist and ex-deputy, who was one of the foremost among those who had proscribed the use of the Latin alphabet for the Albanian language, a Turkish Artillery captain named Irfan Bey, a Major of the Ottoman General Staff, Kemal Effendi, and Lieutenant Kazem Effendi – are reputed to be the instigators of this meaningless but troublesome movement. All of them are men without fortune, yet all of them distributed money with lavish hands.

One may ask with astonishment what rational purpose can lie at the root of this disruptive propaganda. As yet no motive, serious or plausible, has been set forth or hinted at. That the Young Turks who forfeited Albania by their folly cannot hope to regain it by their intrigues, is evident to the dullest apprehension. Geographically, the country is now cut off from the rest of the Ottoman Empire, and politically, there is no bond of union between the two states. As for their common religion, it is indeed outwardly professed by a majority of Albanians, but even these are split up into hostile sects whose adepts are amongst the deadliest enemies of Turkish rule and of the Orthodox Moslem faith. One plausible explanation is that the Young Turks, acting as the instrument of others who are eager to provoke pan-Balkan troubles for the purpose of rectifying their own frontiers, have embarked on a scheme which they fondly imagine will afford them an opportunity of repeating in respect of other portions of their lost territory, the venture which they so successfully carried out in Adrianople. Another is suggested by the Turkish press organ *Tanin*, namely, that Djemal Bey, who was a prisoner of the Serbs and went straight to Albania on being released, may be acting on behalf of a section of the Slavs.

In a word, every man's hand is against Albania, which before it can be properly kneaded into a compact political community and accoutred for self-defence, has become the battleground of Serbs, Montenegrins, Young Turks, and Greeks, as in the dreary days of yore. Called to life by sundry agencies, like a mummy resuscitated by the alchemy of a wonder-working magician, it was at once turned adrift among beasts of prey eager to devour it, with no serviceable weapon of defence, and now it is in danger of lapsing into chaos.

Turning from external difficulties to the internal situation, we are faced with a set of conditions the like of which has probably never been witnessed in modern Europe. To characterise the resulting state as chaotic is to give but a faint idea of the mad *chassez croisez* of chiefs who have no subordinates; of subordinates who are at the beck and call of numerous disunited chiefs; of a cabinet thwarted by an International Commission of Control, which calls for its abolition and volunteers to govern in its stead; of zealous and well-meaning Dutch officers checkmating both commission and cabinet, obtaining supreme power and bending the king to their will; of an Austrian political adviser pulling the rudder in one direction and an Italian political adviser giving the wheel a turn in the other; of the head of the government and of three ministries being suddenly roused out of sleep at dead of night and bombarded with mountain guns without being condemned or accused of any crime or misdemeanour; of a misinformed sovereign despatching artillery and quick-firing guns against a body of malcontents who solemnly declare that they came only as petitioners; of a court and cabinet fleeing for refuge to the foreign warships from a town which, as they thought, was about to be given up to fire and the sword. Albania would seem to have become a vast bedlam, of which Durazzo is the special ward for the violent and most dangerous inmates. It is not to be supposed that the upright intentions or good faith of any of those bodies or individuals is being impugned. Far from it. They are all well-meaning, honourable, and feverishly active in pursuit of conflicting aims. Each one is bent on saving Albania from the anarchy into which the ill-considered doings of the others are plunging it. Each of them is convinced that there is a panacea for the ills of the country, but that before it can be applied, the realm must be purged from the disastrous influences of the rest.

The pathetic side of this strange phenomenon lies in the circumstance that every one of these individuals, like the fly on the wheel, fancies that he is the source of any progress or movement that can be produced, whereas in truth what goes on outside the country is alone of any moment, and these actors are but playing with branches, the roots of which are hidden without and are watered or withered by forces to which neither they nor the population has access. They have yet to learn how limited is the reach of the internal agencies.

By these factitious contrivances, a problem eminently easy in itself has become well-nigh insoluble. The Albanians are among the most chivalrous and also the most docile people in Europe, once the chords are touched which alone can evoke a response in their hearts. But one must understand the peculiar workings of the national mind and set before it such motives as have power to stir it. And most of the bodies and persons charged with the work of ruling over the people and of modifying their political and social structure, know them only through the uncouth phraseology of the interpreter or the coloured medium of disjointed reports. I was struck with instances of this disqualification on more than one occasion. After the fighting of Saturday, May 23, the Commission of Control proposed to the insurgents that they should give up their wounded for medical treatment, which was available only at Durazzo. But the offer was politely declined. Then adroit feelers were thrown out to elicit the number of their casualties, but with no result. This extraordinary reticence was noticed and commented by the international statesmen, some of whom drew fanciful conclusions from it. The natives, on the contrary, felt no surprise at a reserve which they know to be in accordance with the secular usages of their countrymen.

The Albanian people may roughly be likened to sharp, rough stones of many shapes and sizes, taken from an old Roman structure. They may still serve to form a comfortable modern dwelling provided they are cut and fashioned under the direction of builders who know the sort of edifice they are going to construct and how to carry out the plan. But if in lieu of qualified builders and workmen you set a number of watchmakers, tulip-growers, or hatters to do the work, and if these are disagreed as to whether a palace, a church, or a row of cottages is wanted, the chances of any useful or ornamental building coming out of their experiment will be slender.

Among the many strange politico-social phenomena that press their unwontedness upon the observant foreign student of Albania, two or three are entitled to supreme prominence in the minds of those who are set to govern the nation and to smooth its march from mediaeval twilight towards the dazzling glare of contemporary civilisation. The feudal ordering of a large section of the people, their canine fidelity to their chiefs, their ingrained reverence for hereditary authority, the feuds of the clans among themselves, the absence of any regular machinery for the prevention or detection of crime, for the trial and punishment of criminals, and for the security of life and property, and the alleged necessity of the vendetta as a substitute for this, are characteristic traits which must of necessity impart to the future state in its initial phase, a conformation, social, and political, wholly unlike that of any other nation. And it behoves those whose work it is to fuse these clans into an organism and keep ward over its development, to take due account of these ancient survivals. Common sense tells us that it would be folly to attempt to abolish them summarily, or to expect a rude people whose habits of life and modes of thought and feeling are those of the twelfth century, to plunge all at once into the twentieth.

In the light of these axioms, many of the preliminaries of government which run counter to them and have already been established are provoking acrid criticism among Albanians and in especial the Western style and splendid isolation of the court. The king and queen, it is argued, live in a palace aloof from their people. Their surroundings are foreign, their habits and customs are those of the court of Oldenburg or Mecklenburg-Strelitz, their language is German or French, their whole atmosphere is alien, and the prop and stay of their throne Austrian, Italian, or international. That the natives should notice these things and grumble at them is perhaps natural, but the strictures which they ground upon them are unwarranted. Less gratuitous is the criticism that the general trend of the court is calculated to keep it at too great a distance from the bulk of the nation. Natives of education and experience like the Finance Minister Philip Nogga, who contributed materially to bring Prince Wied to Albania, hold that the court which might with advantage be taken as a model is that of Montenegro. Albania's chief should conceive his rule as that of a paternal lord invested with great power, wielding it prudently for the good of his people, with whom it should be his care to identify himself in every feasible way. Thus, it would strengthen the bonds of union between them and him if he appeared before them from time to time in the national costume, visited their towns and villages, invited their chiefs to his palace, displayed an interest in their minor affairs, and made them feel that he has become one of themselves.

I record these views as worth noting without acquiescence or dissent[16].

What strikes me as a noteworthy factor in the present situation, and an element in the relations between ruler and people, is the bitter disillusion which has ensued upon three months of Prince William's reign. This, too, is a grievance for which the German prince can hardly be made answerable. But the writ of reason does not run among a primitive people like the Arnauts, whose empire is entirely of sentiment. The tidings that the tribes and clans, whose life since the dawn of history had been one continuous battle, were now to be

---

[16] These and other valuable suggestions were embodied in a detailed programme which M. Philip Nogga drew up for the Prince zu Wied and presented to him in Germany. Writing with the limited knowledge of an outsider, I feel disposed to regard these recommendations as calculated to solve most of the problems which the prince was free to tackle.

advanced to the dignity of an independent realm, made them conscious of a new fibre in their moral constitution, and gave rise to fantastic hopes and infantine expectations. The common people – who had been as serfs, living and dying in the mountains for their hereditary chieftains, or hewing wood and drawing water for their Beys and Pashas in the valleys – pictured to themselves their king as a sort of demiurge, who would lead them triumphantly against mighty enemies and bestow upon them copious spoils of war, or fancied that his fiat would transmute their misery into happiness and their serfdom into a millennium. The semi-educated groups who had lived abroad or become inoculated with the pseudo constitutional principles disseminated by the Young Turks during the first phase of their evolution, at once brought into gaudy prominence their new-fangled notions and beheld visions of the romance of statesmanship in which they would play a commanding part.

Prince Wilhelm, even before his arrival, became the symbol and the instrument of this impending metamorphosis which everybody expected as a certainty. But each section and individual construed it as the realisation of his own particular ideals. The king, like the manna in the desert, was to satisfy the individual longings of each. And the disappointment that followed his accession to the throne was general and bitter. Alone a section of the Moslems in the south and centre, mistrustful of all change, and apprehending that however cheerless their lot had been, the shifting of the political balance might easily make it worse – put forward the demand that their new ruler should be chosen from among their own creed. And for a time, they believed that this desire would be fulfilled, for their most puissant representative, Essad Pasha, seconded their petition, contending that, as the majority of the inhabitants were followers of Mohammed, their ruler also ought to be a Moslem. When, however, the powers decided that the throne should be bestowed on a Christian prince, Essad, aware that protests would be unavailing, made a merit of necessity and pilgrimaged to Germany to invite Prince Wilhelm zu Wied to don the thorny crown of Albania. Many of the Mussulmans were dismayed at the prospect which an overwrought imagination, stimulated by artful suggestions from without, conjured up before them. And against Essad, they uttered an ominous *tu quoque* and fulminant execrations, which intimated that his crime would be followed by condign punishment.

But the group of Mohammedans who thought and behaved thus was small and their opposition negligible. What subsequently made it appear formidable was the admixture of the Young Turkish element, which carnè into the country for the express purpose of disaffecting them towards the prince and played on the religious chord as the most likely one to evoke the requisite response. This propaganda, which took effect only on a few *hodjas*, may have misled the foreign officials at Durazzo, who at once talked of wild religious fanaticism, seriously apprehended a religious war, and unwittingly caused a panic in the capital.

Religious fanaticism is practically unknown in Albania. There is too little real religion available for the purpose. It is lost labour to fan embers if there is no fuel for a fire. Catholicism and Islam became largely diluted with Albanian customs before being assimilated by this most conservative people in Europe. Each of the three faiths, Catholicism, Orthodoxy, and Islam had to stoop before it could conquer.

None of them succeeded in doing away with the vendetta which is still answerable for three-fourths of the deaths of the Catholic mountaineers. A large percentage of the Mohammedans belong to a sect which the Turks abhor as semi-Christian. The adepts of this denomination, some of whose members I have myself questioned, leave the faces of their women uncovered, eat pork, drink wine, reject the dogmas of creation and a future life, and the initiated among them hold a body of doctrine which may be roughly characterised as pantheistic materialism. They are the religious offshoot of the Janissaries, and their annals, still hardly known, are calculated to shed an interesting light on some of the salient events of Turkish history. Among other doctrines of the Bek Tashis [Bektashis], that of the equal value of all religions occupies a prominent place. It is worth noting parenthetically that Essad Pasha's family, the Toptanis, has always been at daggers drawn with the Bektashis, of whom not a trace is to be found in those towns or districts like Shiak, Tirana, Kavaya, where his power was preponderant. The Bektashis have ever been the enemies of the Beys and Pashas.

The Catholics of the northern mountains are of all Albanian Christians, the most submissive to their clergy, to whom they pay dues in kind. But they are still more devoted to their chiefs, and when Prenk Bib Doda's father quarrelled with the bishops, he allowed his men to plunder and maltreat them, which they did with a will until the church dignitaries knuckled down and asked for mercy. Among the Catholic troops faithful to the king are many Moslems, while a considerable percentage of Catholics is to be found among the

Mohammedan insurgents of the centre, who were supposed to be ready to put the Christians of Durazzo to the sword.

In view of these things, there would seem to lie little doubt that many of those who are at the head of affairs in the capital of Albania have yet to learn the history and the psychology of the people whose destinies they are vainly endeavouring to shape.

If, then, we eliminate religion as one of the decisive factors of the internal Albanian problem, we find as residue two elements which lie at its deepest roots: on the one hand, the feudal pyramid with the faithful clans as its base and the chieftains invested with absolute authority, including sometimes power of life and death, as its apex, and on the other hand, a strong natural current set against the power of the Beys and Pashas, and a longing to dispossess them of the land, both tendencies fomented by the doctrines and the practices of the Mohammedan Bek Tashis [Bektashis] and the Christian nationalists of the extreme wing.

Such in general outline is the rude, benighted people whom Europe's fiat is to turn into a united nation with a central government and a royal head. Now, it seems clear that one condition of success is that the continuity of this primitive tribal system shall not be broken suddenly, but it is equally clear that it should be swayed, directed, gradually modified, and utilised at every stage of the process as an efficacious instrument of good government[17]. But a vast transformation such as this presupposes the supreme control of one strong and free man. Only a leader gifted with clear, direct vision,

---

[17] The way to approach this delicate task, and perhaps to accomplish it, was pointed out by M. Nogga in the memorandum already alluded to, which he gave the Prince *zu* Wied before his accession.

who puts his heart in his work, is alive to its difficulties, is capable of wide surveys, quick resolve, and tenacity of purpose – a man who is not afraid even of making a mistake – is needed to lead the people out of their camp of mediaeval ideas, barbarous customs, and antiquated traditions into the open air and fierce light of twentieth-century civilisation. The Albanians respect power and yield themselves readily to the fascination of personal strength and prowess. A king who moved among them, made their interests his, entered into their joys and sorrows, settled their disputes and showed that he was one of themselves, would win their sympathies, command their respect, and gradually move into the position now occupied by their hereditary chieftains. And the achievement of this feat might have been accelerated by associating real power, power like that of Prenk Bib Doda and Essad Pasha, with posts of responsibility in the government. In this way, a salutary principle of fermentation would have been introduced into this Olla Podrida of contrary currents and conflicting strivings. That the present ruler has not fulfilled those conditions is a fact; that he is incapable of fulfilling them is hardly more than a surmise. He can plead with truth that he is not a free agent.

Prince Wilhelm Friedrich Heinrich zu Wied was raised to the throne of Albania on grounds of a negative rather than a positive order, which had little in common with the considerations that would have weighed with an elector whose principal aim was to adjust means to ends. Physically, he is the ideal man for the Albanians – tall, well-built, of commanding presence and dignified gait. His other personal qualities are calculated to command respect or ensure affection. His manners are pleasing, his temper bright and cheerful. He is whole-hearted, generous, and chivalrous, ready to set public business above personal interests and to make heavy sacrifices to duty. Those are all admirable traits in an officer or a civil servant in a well-ordered state. But they are insufficient for a man whose life-task is to dissolve the entire framework of a feudal, disunited people; to put an end to the meaningless war of all against all, which has been the blight of the country for centuries; to make new channels for the energies thus diverted, and to fuse the various groups and units into a harmonious, properly organised state. Besides, it is doubtful whether he possesses independent initiative and adequate will power.

Albania's new ruler, his critics complain, lives in his palace at Durazzo as Dejoces, the Mede, lived in his fantastic stronghold at Ecbatana, a being apart, almost of a different species from that of his subjects. His residence is an oasis in a desert. His surroundings – the people whom he had taken with him and those whom Europe had thrust upon him – are aliens who can seldom tell him what to do and can hardly ever show him how to do it. The whole atmosphere is foreign. And each of these outsiders is jealous of the other and eager to win ascendancy over the inexperienced prince. Their powers, vaguely outlined, overlap; their ambitions have been stretched beyond their legitimate scope, and the upshot is confusion.

Thus, there was an International Commission of Control composed of men actuated by the very best intentions but unable efficaciously to protect the king against his enemies and unwilling to supply the funds needed for the organisation of a band of native troops to protect him. Then there were the Dutch officers whom Europe despatched to organise a corps of gendarmes, and whose extreme zeal, scrupulous attention to minute detail, and impulsive action have been an unending cause of troubles and complications, national and international, ever since, for it was their amazing treatment of Essad Pasha and their unprovoked attack against the petitioners of Shiak and Tirana, who were misnamed insurgents and, at present, perhaps, merit this appellation, that brought government to a standstill and produced the panic in the capital which culminated in the flight of the Royal Family. It was the zealous Dutch officers also who, sacrificing to what they deemed the highest interests of the state the capitulations on the one hand and their duty as subordinates which obliged them to consult the ministry on the other hand, entered the house of an Italian subject, treated him and his acquaintance ungently, seized their papers, placed them under arrest, and then refused to accept the officer's parole and the Italian Minister's guarantee that they would appear before a court of inquiry when called upon. They then referred the matter to the sovereign, whose orders they invoiced as their warrant, and thus involved him in an international quarrel without the solace of a good cause.

The Italian and Austrian Ministers are *ex officio* counsellors to the king, and it is commonly supposed, I know not with how much reason, that the advice of the one is often contrary to that of the other. In the palace, there were two professional political mentors, one an Italian officer named Castoldi, and the other an Austrian named Buchberger. In addition to the abundance of political wisdom supplied by all these bodies and individuals, there was the cabinet and the opposition. The former, under the leadership of Turkhan Pasha, an experienced diplomatist and gentleman of the good old school, advocated a policy of conciliation and prudent opportunism, while the latter consisted of the nationalists, the extreme wing of which was composed of sincere but unripe patriots, impatient to see the great transformation realised, mouthing empty watchwords, descanting on the principles of high politics, and waiting for the moment when the reins of power shall fall to themselves.

All those professional and amateur advisers, none of whom the prince could afford to ignore, were honourable men who would fain regenerate the country as it should, in their opinion, be regenerated. They all cry 'Forwards!' But as each of them has a different direction in mind, the sovereign, uncertain which to take, is distraught and paralysed. All decent semblance of unity is gone. The various authorities, national and international, are engaged in the game of baulking each other, in which they have all been beaten except the Dutch officers, who have had their own way, to the disgust of the others and the detriment of the country. The resources of Albania, economic and other, are being drained to no purpose, and the taproot of the national life seems blighted.

It was a Dutch officer, Colonel Thomson, an honest, hardworking, and loyal man, who first negotiated with the leaders of the Epirote insurgents. He had a direct authorisation[18] from Prince Wilhelm, and only from him, but as soon as he had affected a settlement of their claims, he was disavowed by the cabinet, which then empowered the Commission of Control to come to terms. The Commission of Control went to Corfu and made concessions to the rebels, which the cabinet accepted only with large reserves. These reserves, formulated emphatically in a document signed by all

---

[18] I have read it.

the ministers, were omitted by somebody in the copy which was delivered to the Greeks! Then the Dutch officers refused to obey orders issued by Essad Pasha in his capacity as minister of the interior and titulary war minister. Essad appealed to the king, whom he suspected of leanings towards the Dutch and spoke with uncourtly frankness to His Majesty. The cabinet upheld Essad, and between the latter and the Dutch officers, and in particular Major Slujs, there has been no love lost ever since.

Essad had been a force in the country before the prince's arrival. He was then the spokesman of the orthodox Moslem population, which clamoured for a Moslem sovereign. But, resigning himself to the will of Europe, he journeyed to Newied with the deputation, which invited the prince to rule over Albania. Although this act of patriotic renunciation had cost him his prestige and power among the Mohammedans, he still retained great influence, which he knew how to make the most of. His agents were men devoted to him, *âmes damnées*, who thought no sacrifice too great for their patron. Now, all that Essad Pasha strove for, although a man of vast ambition, was that he should shave the shadow as he had the substance, arid, that this real power should be associated with corresponding rank in the cabinet or the country, canalised and used for the behalf of the nation and its sovereign. He wanted to play a prominent, if not the leading, part. Such, at least, that and nothing more, is my personal impression gathered from various talks I have had with him during the time that he and I lived together. It is, of course, only an impression: and this moderate wish was not grudged to him by Turkhan Pasha, who understood the psychology of the man and perceived how advantageous a bargain the new state and its ruler were making. The prince, too, who is generous and unsuspecting, appears to have trusted his general, or to have dissembled any mistrust which may have been implanted in his mind by stories of Essad's underhand dealings with Mohammedans, secret intelligence with Greeks, Montenegrins, Serbs, Young Turks, and Italians, which were current among his adversaries, and may have been believed by the over-zealous Dutchmen, whose discretion never equalled their zeal.

It was no secret in Durazzo, Scutari, Valona, or Shiak that Essad was being closely watched by the Dutch and their police, some of whom listened too readily to the idle tales spread by interested and venal mischief-makers. To the pasha, it was galling. At last, they claimed to have adequate proofs which satisfied them of the treason of their powerful enemy. But this evidence, if it exists, has never been adduced, nor was the shadowed man apprised of the cloud that hung over him.

Essad Pasha is perhaps the shrewdest man in Albania, and one of the most supple and resourceful. His change of attitude on the question of a Moslem ruler offers an illustration of his opportunism and adaptability. That such a man, after such a sacrifice, should get entangled in a set of conflicting and hopeless movements against the state in which he was playing the first part after the sovereign, is almost inconceivable. He realised that the powers would never accept him as sovereign. He was aware that they would never invite nor recognise a Mohammedan ruler. In a word, for an insurrectionary outbreak there was no goal. And he himself had nothing to gain and everything to lose by dabbling in plots and conspiracies. He is the owner of immense estates, the revenue from which will increase fifty-fold when order is permanently established and normal national life begins. Fidelity to the king was therefore his trump card, and he seems to have played it. The worst that one can lay to his charge – so far as I who know him, but not his accusers, can discern – was a desire to make himself necessary to the prince, a wish to play tile part of a *Grand Seigneur*, which he did to perfection and a natural striving to increase his power and prestige.

His great Catholic rival in the north, Prenk Bib Doda, behaved in a very different way. He, too, exercises unquestioned sway over his followers, who are far more numerous and are kept in more strict subjection than Essad's. But Doda accepted no ministerial post and declined to reside within the royal sphere of attraction. He would gladly lend the Monarch some thousands of his tribesmen, as Ras Michael might have lent a military contingent to Menelik, but he would not become a state organ.

Essad Pasha declared for the new order of things before it was established. Bib Doda holds on to the old and watches with curiosity the prophesied evolution from his conning tower outside.

One could not expect brave and loyal Dutch officers, whose business is the training of gendarmes, to analyse thus closely the psychology of Albania's two great chiefs. They mistrusted Essad and scenting treason, ran him to earth.

Turkhan Pasha, the grand vizier and wise moderator, had just gone to Rome and Buda-Pest, leaving Essad in charge, who was therefore war minister, home secretary, and grand vizier all in one. In Shiak, Tirana, and Kavaya the malcontents who had refused him recruits for the South put their heads together and resolved to lodge a protest with the king against the cabinet and against the puissant war minister, whose power they resented and whose land they coveted. Other elements there also were among them, but neither the names of the primary instigators nor their aims have been ascertained with certitude.

These remonstrants, armed as are all Albanians, were holding a meeting at Shiak one morning, when the king and queen chanced to ride out in that direction. Shiak is a village about an hour's walk from Durazzo. The king noticed with surprise the unwonted aspect of the place, the coming and going of the people, and their look of excitement, and soon afterwards, he found the road barred by a dense throng. Divining the character of the manifestation, he turned his horse's head and galloped back to his capital, disconcerted and out of sorts. And in truth, this was an unpleasant surprise, which should have been spared him. He ought to have been made aware of the ferment among the population and advised not to approach the place at all, or only with a firm purpose to take the bull by the horns and talk plainly with his subjects. Some of his official advisers now hold that if he had continued his ride, he would have been acclaimed by the crowd, whose sullen murmurs would have turned to enthusiasm. This forecast is probably correct. Albanians love a strong man and adore a venturesome one. But neither lack of strength nor lack of enterprise was responsible for his conduct. It was lack of knowledge. He was not prepared or the sight that met his eyes, and stories of underground plottings and infamous treason, which he had listened to perhaps incredulously before, may now have floated through his mind with a deeper tinge of probability. Moreover, whatever proof of intrepidity he may have been ready to give he felt bound to postpone until he was alone.

On this day and the next, I was absent in Kalmetti, the guest of Prenk Bib Doda, so that what then happened I now describe not from personal observation but from the sifted narrative of others. When I vacated my apartments in Essad Pasha's house, he resolved to fit them up for his young Circassian wife, who took possession of them in the afternoon of the eventful day. Unimportant in itself, this circumstance seems to rebut the allegations of those, who allege that he had organised a rising for that night or the next. Until conclusive evidence of this amazing charge is produced and winnowed, I, who knew the pasha, cannot entertain the notion that he was at once stupid, treacherous, and suicidal, as he must have been if this count in the whispered indictment against him were true. Nor is this presumption in his favour weakened by significant allusions to certain supposed antecedents of his which the laxest moralist of the West could neither overlook nor condone. Those alleged misdeeds, if brought home to him, would merely mark him as a man of his race, country, and time. Saturated with peculiar notions and feelings, and equipped with an amoral sense common to the whole nation, which Western nations regard with abhorrence, the ethical quality of his conduct cannot be fairly gauged by no standard but that of his own countrymen. And their moral code often enjoins manslaughter but always condemns treachery.

The king, on his return from Shiak, sent for Essad and called for an explanation of his silence if he knew what was going on, or of his remissness if he was unaware of it. What answer was returned to this pertinent query I have had no means of learning, but I understand that the pasha finally tendered his resignation, which was refused, and then pressed it many times on the king. On the same day, Essad and his rival, Major Slujs, whose relations were those of bitter enemies, met, clashed, and agreed that Durazzo could no longer hold them both. The Dutch officer is said to have roundly accused Essad – who was at that time his chief, as war minister, home secretary, and acting Grand Vizier – of treachery to the prince and treason to the state. Forthwith the pasha sought, out the king, informed him of the altercation and requested him to choose between himself and the Dutchman. The prince, it is stated, intimated his resolve to maintain Essad at his post and to appoint Major Slujs to another part of Albania. The major, it is said, refused to go. A few hours later, however, the king reconsidered his decision and declared for the Dutch officer. But the pasha was not dismissed. On the contrary, the sovereign treated him as minister as late as 8 pm that night. Of this victory gained, it is alleged, by means of grave allegations against the pasha, Essad's rival made the utmost. A *coup de main* was carefully elaborated, of which the effect, and seemingly also the object, was not merely to remove but to humiliate and enrage the one man of power and influence in the service of the king. It was also expected that he would be executed summarily as a traitor. Essad's house was surrounded by armed men. Mountain guns were posted on the heights above it, and orders were issued to the gunners to open fire as soon as the concerted signal was given.

In the dead of the night, a messenger was sent by Major Slujs to the residence of the puissant minister to notify him that the forces of the king were posted below, cannons pointed at the building, and gunners ready to fire, and that he had no choice but to obey his sovereign's orders, which were that all the armed men then on the premises should lay down their weapons. The delegate, finding the gate open, entered and knocked at the door of the bedroom. Essad, in his nightdress, opened it and, with sleepy eyes and astonished look, asked what he wanted. His stupefaction at the answer was intense and unfeigned, but it passed quickly; he complied with the demand and gave the order. His men laid down their arms, and it turned out that, instead of a hundred adherents, he had hardly more than a dozen. Throwing open the window, he leant out to catch a glimpse of what was going on below, and then called out, "Who is in command of the men?"

The answer was, "Major Slujs."

"In that man I have no confidence," exclaimed the pasha. Thereupon, his men snatched up their weapons. Soon afterwards, a shot was fired, which each side now attributes to the other but probably came from Essad's house. On this, the signal was given by the Dutch and the gun launched forth its projectiles. Essad's wife fainted. One of his dependants was killed. Part of the roof of his house was blown away. The boom of cannon and the crack of rifles broke the slumbers of peaceful citizens who rushed out of their homes affrighted.

At this conjuncture, an Italian artillery officer of the reserve, Capt. Moltedo – a man of reckless bravery – appeared on the scene and put an end to what bade fair to become a massacre. Moltedo had only arrived in Durazzo that day to enter upon his duties as commander of the Albanian artillery, to which he had been appointed by the cabinet. Hearing the boom of the camion, he left his house and rushed off to the war minister to inquire what was wrong. Realising what was being done, he advised the pasha to deliver up the weapons to him. The minister complied unhesitatingly, whereupon the

Dutch were notified and the firing ceased. Essad and all the other inmates of the house were arrested.

As yet, the minister had been taxed with no definite crime. He now asked with what offence he was charged and who his accusers were. But to these fair questions, there were no answers. "If I am innocent," he exclaimed, "why have I, who am acting grand vizier, war minister, and home secretary been treated like a desperate criminal? And if I am guilty in the eyes of my sovereign, why am I not given an opportunity to rebut the charges against me?" To this query, there was no answer, not even a reply. Some were for trying and punishing him summarily, others for deporting him. Finally, the latter course was decided on and Essad was taken at about 8 am to an Austrian warship anchored in front of Durazzo. Orders had been given that he was to be conducted to the landing place by a route behind the palace. That route, it is said, was lined with personal enemies of his, impatient to murder him. But Essad insisted on walking in front of the palace, and as he passed, he saluted his sovereign, who returned the greeting. From the Austrian, he was soon transferred to an Italian warship and subsequently conveyed to Italy.

I returned to Durazzo on the following day and found his colleagues dismayed, humiliated, enraged. The conspiracy against him had been hatched so secretly that they had had no inkling of it until the plan was carried out. And they were still ignorant alike of the authors and their motives, nor has the mystery as yet been cleared up. Their questions were met with oracular answers or more significant silence. Their telegrams were suppressed. The Dutch took possession of the Telegraph Office. Nobody knew what surprise was still in store. It was whispered that other ministers who were friends of Essad were also proscribed. The young Dragoman of the Ministry who had been attached by Essad to my person – M. Stavro – was seized, roughly handled, and thrown into the filthiest hole of the filthy Turkish prison. He besought his captors to allow the place to be cleansed of some of the ordure that covered the floor. His request was rejected, with jibes. Next day, he was set free, and the Dutch Major, with whom he had often transacted business for the government, apologised to him and hoped he would forgive and forget. On the following day, the same major had him seized in the street and commanded him to give up Essad's cipher. He answered that it had never been in his possession, that it was always kept by the secretary. He was told he must go back to prison until he gave it up, and as he knew nothing about it, he was once more thrown into the loathsome cesspool. There he found the secretary, who informed him that the cipher had already boon given up to the Dutch and sealed by them. Soon afterwards, he was released and solaced with fresh apologies. Now at last, he was free, they told him. A day or two later, however, he was once more seized and entombed in the pestilent black hole of the Turkish prison, where he was kept for eleven days without trial or accusation – by order of the Dutch officers. A short autobiography of Essad, composed by himself for me, was among the papers seized. And neither the cabinet nor I have been able to obtain possession of it ever since.

Thus, bereft of power and saddled with responsibility, the ministers had no choice but to tender their resignation, which they did unanimously. The king demanded time for reflection and requested them meanwhile to carry on the current business of their respective departments. But the current business continued to be done by the Dutch and others, without even the knowledge of the cabinet. M. Nogga, the finance minister, who throughout these days of utter anarchy preserved a cool head and gave sound advice to his colleagues and the king, pressed upon the latter the necessity of instituting a court of inquiry which should investigate the charges against Essad and ascertain the origin and justification of the high-handed way in which he was treated. But no court of inquiry was appointed, no justification attempted, no statement made. Privately, it was admitted that there was no evidence worthy of the name against the fallen minister!

Seeing itself thus reduced to become a screen for doings of a lawless character and disastrous tendency, the cabinet, having waited some days longer, repaired in a body to the palace and handed in a written request to be formally relieved of functions which were being actually discharged by irresponsible persons. The king returning the same answer as before, the ministers announced their inability to cover any longer with their names the fitful freaks of unknown individuals. That was Friday night, May 22. A few days before this, the king had sent for and received 120 Catholic Malissores from the North to guard his palace and person. The Italian Minister doubted the wisdom of this measure and said so. The Dutch officers, without consulting the cabinet or the Commission of Control, despatched these men in the middle of the night to the camp of the malcontents, with orders to occupy Shiak and Tirana. The Malissores demurred at first and then obeyed unwillingly, on the grounds that they were too few for a military expedition and had come to Durazzo in their rich embroidered costumes, which made becoming uniforms for palace guards but were unfitted for soldiers in the field. But the Dutch would take no excuse and led the warriors to Shiak, where they were not molested. They were accompanied by a number of volunteers, including some foreigners with a taste for adventure. It was then 5 am, Saturday, May 23.

Seeing that the attitude of the villagers of Shiak was not aggressive, the order was given to continue the march to Tirana. It was disobeyed by the Malissores, who refused to advance further. When the other members of the expedition had climbed the hill above Shiak, then, and only then, did the bullets begin to whistle past them. Their gun was taken, their own friends in Durazzo misdirecting their artillery fire, killed and wounded several of them, the villagers took about 130 prisoners and the remainder returned to Durazzo, leaving their gun behind.

The amazing tactics which had led to these deplorable results exasperated the ministers, bewildered the Commissioners of Control, sent the foreign diplomatists flying to the palace, and engendered a feeling of insecurity in the capital. People argued that if the safety of the city depended upon officers with so little judgment and upon men with so little discipline, it was obviously at the mercy of any band of resolute rebels who cared to take it.

After this, the capital was indeed at the mercy of the rebels, who, if they entertained the designs attributed to them, might now have executed them without resistance. And as no doubt was entertained by the king's trusted advisers that the capture of Durazzo was their main object, a panic ensued of the kind that seizes upon Christians who are about to fall into the hands of ruthless Chinese rebels or infuriated Bashi Bazouks. Helter-skelter, foreigners of distinction, men, women, and children, rushed to the landing place and fled to the warships. The foreign ministers, convinced that a massacre was at hand, urged on then-lagging countrymen. In hot haste, trunks and boxes were carried from the palace and the houses. Groups of men and women, seared to death, ran hither and thither, not knowing what they said or did. Extreme nationalists, expecting no mercy from the rebels, asked for asylum on board Italian war vessels. The scenes of that memorable day supply an instructive object-lesson for the study of the psychology of the crowd.

Meanwhile, the reports made to the king were alarming. He was assured that the insurgents were already within half an hour of the city. And the statement was quite true, but it might have been uttered with equal truth the day before, or even earlier, for they were not marching but only remaining in positions which they had held for days. Subsequently, indeed, they asseverated that their intention had been to depute some spokesmen to the king with a request that their grievances should be considered and redressed, and they complained that the king's officers had gone out to them with rifles and guns and made war on them without warning or ultimatum. The prince was also informed that the 'advancing army' consisted of thousands of well-organised troops, fanaticised to frenzy by unknown agitators, and that at any moment, they might enter the city and put the inhabitants to the sword. The marines, it was added, would have to be withdrawn and the city left to its fate. Hence, it behoved the Royal Family to accept the hospitality of the warships betimes.

This advice must have been repugnant to Prince Wilhelm, who, whatever else may be said of him, is an officer who knows no fear and sets duty above life. But what was duty? If your guide in a pitch-dark cave tells you to jump and adds that the height is five feet, what can you do but carry out his behest, even though your eyes seem to assure you that there is no break in the level ground? True, there were other advisers who advocated a different course. Finance Minister Nogga adjured the king to remain, declared that the insurgents harboured no blood-thirsty designs; that their number hardly amounted to more than three hundred men; that he would answer for it they would acclaim the king if he went out to them, and that in no case was there any ground for alarm. In the interests of the nation and his dynasty, therefore, he implored the king not to quit the city. A member of the Commission of Control urged the same arguments and proffered the same advice. The young monarch was bewildered. Alone he would have stayed where he was, but the queen was resolved to remain with him. Finally, in order to induce her to quit the palace, he yielded to the insistence of the more influential counsellors and decided to withdraw to one of the Italian warships.

This was the most unlucky course he could have chosen. But a little forethought would have sufficed to counteract its most mischievous effects and to mitigate the remainder. The king might, for instance, have announced his intention to escort his consort to the Italian warship and to return an hour or two later. He would then have an opportunity of seeing for himself which of the two conflicting accounts of the alleged impending danger was correct and his departure would not be construed as flight. To the success of this plan, however, an indispensable condition was that the servants should be left in the palace and the flag kept flying. And these precautions were neglected. Every inmate joined the exodus, cooks, washerwomen, electricians, everybody. The shutters were then closed and, lest anyone should doubt that the king had really gone, and gone for good, his zealous adherents hauled down the royal flag!

The marines, barring access to the palace, had shut off the people of the city from this interesting spectacle. The house in which I live stands beside the palace and commands a view of the royal residence, the landing place, and the warships. From my balcony, I witnessed the unwilling departure of the Royal Family, and the spontaneous flight of the ministers and others who set a high price on their own lives and gratuitously credited the villagers with the instincts of ferocious savages. The king and queen passed out amid the ominous silence of the Malissores and other faithful tribesmen in whose brains no intelligible picture of the day's occurrences had yet been limned. Away in the offing hundreds of men, women, and children were huddled together on small torpedo boats where they spent the night in utter discomfort. All the cabinet ministers except M. Nogga departed. He and his wife refused to be separated from their fellow-citizens, to be specially protected by marines or to believe the villagers of Shiak and Tirana capable of massacring their unarmed countrymen.

Soon after this impressive scene was enacted, the 'bloodthirsty' insurgents delegated their spokesman to Durazzo for the purpose of talking matters over with the Commission of Control. This body itself, however, was already on the way out to Shiak and met the delegates. A conference for the following day was agreed upon and peace fell upon Durazzo. Two and a half hours after his departure, the king returned to the city, but his palace was empty and dark and there were no servants. Lamps from M. Nogga's room and mine were lent to him until the electricians arrived. A feeble attempt was then got up to launch the version that the king had never meant to abandon his city, but in the face of tell-tale facts, which could neither be denied nor explained away, this flimsy theory was abandoned. It is not necessary. The king's action can be vindicated on other grounds. It was an error of judgment, for which most of the responsibility lies with others.

The ensuing events may be summarily recounted. It was tardily discovered that the fanatical monsters who had struck fear to the hearts of the population were necessitous peasants who had nothing to eat or drink and scarcely anything to protect them from wind and weather. They had hoped the king's arrival in Durazzo would usher in halcyon days and enable them to lead lives worth living, but they had been bitterly disappointed. Since then, they had been told that a Moslem Sovereign would have affected what the Christian prince never attempted, and that badly off as they now were, far worse things awaited them if the present *régime* endured. Hence, they demanded the dethronement of Prince Wilhelm and the accession of a Mohammedan prince. To the expostulations and suasion of the Commissioners of Control, they replied that blood having been shed by the king there was feud between him and them, feud which was abiding. But they protested that they were resolved to keep to the defensive and would not attack Durazzo. They gave up all their prisoners and behaved towards the commission with marked courtesy. The prisoners on their return lauded the insurgents for their consideration towards them which in many cases bordered on tenderness. Of religious fanaticism, there were no symptoms.

Among the rebels, there are many Christians, just as there is a large percentage of Moslems among their adversaries.

On the advice of one set of his prompters, the king, as soon as he was back in the palace, dismissed the Malissores to their homes in the North. A few days later, he recalled them, together with six hundred more. This latter measure was adopted on the advice of his Minister Nogga who, from this time onward, appears to have won, as he had long deserved, the king's full confidence. Nogga's programme now began to be carried out by instalments. The Commission of Control, however, objected very strongly to the recall of the Malissores which had been decided and effected without their approval or knowledge, and they prophesied that sinister consequences would speedily ensue. Some of the foreign diplomatists concurred in this judgment, and the king was advised to send the highlanders away before they became restive. But this time, the sovereign held his ground.

As soon as the Commission of Control had had its decisive talk with the insurgents and announced that it had failed to induce them to disperse, M. Nogga proposed that the Malissores, who had all been meanwhile enrolled as gendarmes, should be equipped and sent simultaneously with contingents from Alessio, Fieri, and Elbassan to surround, without actually attacking, the rebels, with whom negotiations might he profitably begun. In this, the king acquiesced. But once more, the Commission of Control, which would fain abolish the cabinet and administer the country, opened its mind to him on the subject of the dangers involved in such an enterprise which, to their thinking, connoted civil war, bitter religions strife, disaffection, and probably defeat, followed by anarchy. 'Fatal' was the adjective used by one of the commissioners to the king to characterise the consequences he foretold. And when Finance Minister Nogga requested the commission to open a credit for the equipment of the native forces, he was told that it could not be done because it was needless and baleful seeing that the insurgents, if time enough were given them, would return to their homes peaceably. The minister insisted, pointing out that as the powers had refused to send international troops to defend the prince and restore order in the country, it would ill become them to withhold from the prince's government the funds which would enable it to do the work itself. After heated discussions, the commission yielded but not before the ministers had intimated that they must lay the matter before the sovereign and draw the practical consequences from the refusal. And now the plan put forward by Nogga is accepted, to bring tribesmen from Fieri, Alessio, Elbassan, isolate the disaffected villages, and try the virtue of suasion reinforced by a deterrent, on the malcontents. The command of the forces has been given to Colonel Thomson, a Dutch officer, whose dismissal is now demanded for his unjustifiable breach of international law in arresting two Italian subjects.

To sum up: Albania is for the moment a political Slough of Despond in which nationalists, Catholics, Moslems, Bek Tashis, Beys, pashas, demi-serfs, European commissioners, cabinet ministers, Dutch officers, foreign diplomatists, insurgents, and gendarmes are floundering about *pêle-mêle,* not knowing what they or their neighbours are doing. And so long as the causes of this chaotic tangle continue to be operative, the effects will necessarily continue to make themselves felt. To attempt to build up a self-sufficing state under the actual conditions most of which Europe has deliberately imposed is like trying to twist a rope of sand. Albania in its present plight may be likened to a drop of water imprisoned in a crystal, complete in itself, but shut up in a hard, impassable medium where it can neither expand into vapour nor harden into ice. And Prince Wilhelm's function is to gaze at this crystal steadfastly and feast his soul on the visions and potentialities that unfold themselves to his inner sight as he contemplates it. It is not given him to penetrate the crystal, neither can he modify the water-drop.

E. J. Dillon

The Contemporary Review, July–December 1914

Greece And Turkey Drifting Into War

Greece and Turkey went to war in 1912 without any such overpowering motive as that which determined the Slav peoples of the Balkan Peninsula to take the field. Their differences were few and of a kind which might have been settled to the satisfaction of both without an appeal to arms. The conflict that finally broke out between them was a consequence of that fatal short-sightedness which characterised the Young Turks in the conduct of all their public business, domestic and international, during the first period of their activity. Acquainted only partially with the terms of a problem and unable to take into account certain of its decisive factors, they strove to impose a solution which it would not bear and by so striving exposed their country to dangers, the extent of which they had no means of gauging. Perhaps the most striking illustration of these leaps in the dark is afforded by the history of their relations with Greece, which culminated in the war. That history is curious, instructive, and characteristic. It has never been written, nor even hinted at. Only a very few of the interested parties have any inkling of it. For the present, it may suffice to say that it saddles the cabinet of Said Pasha with one of the heaviest responsibilities any government has ever had to bear.

It is curious to note that of all the belligerents of the Balkan Campaign, those two states, whose quarrel was then but surface-deep, have kept up hostilities of set purpose ever since. True, there have been no battles, naval or military, but short of this, they set themselves to injure each other by every available means and even at the risk of damaging their own interests. In this, it must be admitted that the Turks have been the aggressors. And the circumstance that they did not formally declare war is to be ascribed solely to impotency which they have been straining every national sinew and muscle to overcome. In this striving, they had made such headway that in the latter half of June, level-headed statesmen deemed it possible to fix approximately the date of the Greco-Turkish war of 1914. The time-limits within which they confidently expected it were between the last decade of July and the end of the first half of August.

Both Turkey and Greece, having received their loans from France, bid against each other for Dreadnoughts, purchased submarines and torpedo boats, stored ammunition, and requisitioned the best of their sea-faring population to man them, for the struggle would have been confined to water, Greece and Turkey not possessing coterminous territories. This was reckoned a serious disadvantage for the Ottoman Government, Turkey being for the moment inferior to Greece as a sea power, whereas her army can look back upon a glorious past, and when again at its best, may count upon a still more brilliant future. Only if Bulgaria could have been moved to throw in her lot with the Osmanli in a campaign against Greece, would it be possible to utilise the land army.

Efforts were put forth to induce King Ferdinand's Government to make common cause with its late foe, but in vain. The Bulgarian people had had enough of wars and too much of native diplomacy. And if King Ferdinand's Government had been rash enough to call the soldiers to the colours, it is probable that the response would have been insubordination. For those reasons, the seemingly impending collision between Greece and Turkey would necessarily have taken the shape of a naval campaign.

Growth of Greco-Turkish Animosity

The Greco-Turkish quarrel, which, in 1912, was flimsy, took deep root after the peace of Bucharest. From a question of territorial claims, which was two years ago, it became a race struggle envenomed by religious fanaticism, political chauvinism, greed of land, and personal passion. Greece could neither assimilate nor nationalise the Mohammedans of her newly acquired provinces, nor could Turkey trust the Hellenic elements in the territory she had saved from annexation. Each state was thus confronted with the like problem – how to protect itself from the enemy in its camp.

Among the heterogeneous ethnic ingredients of the Ottoman Empire are over two million of Hellenic subjects whose language, traditions, and culture are Greek. These people constitute the most important economic force in the country. Trade and commerce are in their hands. They are the best, and in most parts of Turkey the only, seamen. Even in such big cities as Smyrna, where four-sevenths of the inhabitants are Hellenes, public life would be at a complete standstill if the Greeks were to strike work. Banks, bakeries, cafés, restaurants, shops would have to close, trains would cease to run, steamers could neither take nor discharge cargoes. In a word, the whole economic mechanism of the place would be stopped.

During the Balkan campaign, this influential population sympathised heartily with Turkey's enemies, who were the allies of the Greeks. And, unhappily for the Turks, a certain proportion of her own soldiers were Hellenes. Whenever possible, this hostile element aided and abetted the Christian invaders by every means in their power, and the means in their power were sometimes enough to turn the scale in favour of the allies. Thus, in Macedonia, the Hellenes received the Bulgarians with open arms and enabled them to capture important places by dispatching a mere *posse* of thirty or even fifteen soldiers, while employing the bulk of their armies where they were most needed. To the soul of the patriotic Turk, the necessity of thus harbouring domestic enemies was as gall and wormwood. The empire could never be guaranteed against treachery so long as this danger endured. Now all the coast of Asia Minor is inhabited by Hellenes, the direct descendants of the colonists who were settled there in the days of Pericles, and long before. And in the hearts of these Hellenes patriotic fire burns even more fiercely than in those of their brethren of the kingdom of Hellas.

The bitterness engendered by the sayings and doings of these unwilling Ottoman subjects can well be imagined. A patriotic Turk, when he learned that his Hellenic fellow subjects had been to Greece to serve as soldiers in the army there, or that a tithe was spontaneously paid and regularly collected by the Orthodox priests for the Greek fleet, may well have felt incensed beyond endurance. No war was possible on equal terms so long as the Hellenic section of the population remained animated by these sentiments.

The climax of indignation was reached when Greece, having annexed the islands of Chios, Mitylene, and Samos, which command the coast of Asia Minor, had her claim to keep them allowed by Europe. Naval and military experts had declared the possession of these islands and more particularly of Chios and Mitylene, absolutely indispensable to the effective defence of the coast of the mainland. When I was with Abdullah Pasha in Boudja and Smyrna in 1912, he explained to me the importance which he and his staff attached to Chios, which at that time was Turkish, for the protection of Smyrna. At one spot, the steaming distance between the two places is hardly more than half an hour. And as the population of the islands, as well as that of the coast, was exclusively Hellenic, Turkey's plight was pitiable. Her military and naval authorities were faced by the insoluble problem of defending the coast, which was inhabited by implacable, resourceful, and numerous foes, against a neighbour which could command the gratuitous services of those foes and possessed over and above strategic positions of decisive importance in the adjoining islands, and her political leaders were confronted with the equally insoluble problem of maintaining correct relations with a nation which openly avowed its resolve to possess itself one day of the coast of Asia Minor and, if possible, of Constantinople as well.

It soon became evident to everyone with an eye for international politics that the only possible relations between Greece and Turkey were superlatively good or bad. The two peoples must become fast friends, or remain rancorous enemies, biding their time and preparing to cross swords. Between those alternatives, no middle course can be steered.

A Regenerate Young Turk And A Desperate Problem

Now this condition of affairs was intolerable to Turkey, whose only hope of national existence and growth is consolidation and who has but this last chance of realising it. And consolidation under these circumstances was well-nigh unattainable. The most dangerous enemies a state can have are those of its own household. The Young Turks, who had begun their political activity as theorists and visionaries, and had committed disastrous mistakes during the first years of their rule, appear to have learned much by their bitter experience. Among other things, they have perceived the necessity of moving slowly, of taking account of obstacles, of making compromises, and of looking upon politics as the art of the possible. Accordingly, they have shaken off their theories and set themselves to operate with and among realities. They seem minded to begin at the beginning and to do what is still possible to attenuate the consequences of their past errors. Those among them who are endowed by nature with the gift of leadership are rising to the occasion, and deploying a degree of resourcefulness, foresight, and prudence which cannot be too highly commended. Talaat Bey, for example, who began his career as a fiery spirit, impatient of opposition, ardent for the immediate transformation of the nation and its adjustment to the new conditions – he was known as the Jacobin of the Young Turks – has of late displayed a just appreciation of the situation worthy of a trained politician. And the striking proofs he has given since then of his capacity for seeing events in correct perspective and for organisation on a comprehensive scale bid fair to win for him a place among the statesmen of Europe. He and his colleagues have set zealous and valiant hands to the arduous task of kneading all the elements of the Ottoman Empire into a homogeneous nation and reconstructing the Musulman State on entirely new and more European foundations without impairing its character or wounding the susceptibilities of its constituent parts. That, at any rate, is the professed ideal.

This task is beset with hindrances, of which the most redoubtable is a direct outcome and necessary consequence of the nature of a Musulman State, which in principle is theocratic, like that of the ancient Hebrews. The social and political fabric is grounded on the doctrines of the Koran. Consequently, these precepts, together with the duties and rights which flow from them, bind together in a single community the partisans of the faith who acknowledge them, while all others are implicitly eliminated. That is why the Christians of various nationalities have always enjoyed a large measure of self-government under the direction of their ecclesiastical chiefs, of whom the Ecumenical Patriarch of Constantinople is by far the most influential. This creation of a state within the state has survived the constitution and is now a fruitful source of the most serious obstacles to the work of regeneration which the present government has so energetically taken in hand. The average Musulman still considers his Christian fellow-subject as a man of another law, of a different political organisation, as an outsider whose interests are at variance with those of the Musulman State. On the other hand, the spiritual chief, say of the Greeks, by way of protesting against a legislative measure or a political grievance inflicted by the authorities or by a section of the population, has only to publish a decree, and all the schools and churches of the Greeks in the empire are forthwith closed, and the Hellenic citizens are filled with bitter resentment against their fellow subjects and their common rulers.

To dislodge this formidable obstacle to progress and consolidation is a task to achieve which will tax all the ingenuity, energy, and perseverance of the men who are at present at the head of the government. It is not impossible to accomplish it, but only the highest qualities of statesmanship deployed with unflagging perseverance can reckon upon final success. The fulfilment of this condition presupposes dictatorial power invested in a statesman capable of devising a programme, possessed of influence and prestige enough to carry it out, gifted with sufficient moral courage to swerve from it now and again as shifting circumstances may require, and able to kindle the sentiment that shall render it palatable.

If Turkey be possessed of such a leader in this her day of stress and danger, his name will probably be found to be Talaat Bey, who, owing little to training and everything to inborn qualities, has shown a rare capacity for gauging the trend of currents and the bearings of events, profiting by his own mistakes, taking long views, and adjusting his means to changing conditions. It is largely owing to him that the sentiments and ideas which were formerly accumulated and stored by the Secret Committee are now embodied by a responsible government which can understand the need of schooling them into acceptable measures. Speaking personally, as one who took part in the negotiations, the failure of which precipitated the Balkan War, and also as one who criticised Talaat Bey and his colleagues unsparingly during the early part of their political activity, I may say that if he had been in power in the summer of 1912, and if he could have imposed his will on his colleagues, the Balkan campaign would probably never have broken out.

Why the Turks Hate and Persecute Their Hellenic Fellow Subjects

That war and the diplomatic patchwork that followed upon it were the parents of international evils of which Europe has not yet beheld the last nor perhaps the most redoubtable. The Turks who saw themselves deprived of the islands which they deemed indispensable to the defence of the coast of Asia Minor, and saw that coast inhabited by men of Hellenic culture and sentiment, whose political dream was the annexation of Smyrna to the kingdom of Greece, were, so to say, baited to savageness. A number of them under an influential member of the committee organised a system of boycott such as had been practised against the Austrians when Bosnia and Herzegovina were definitely sundered from Turkey. Every Hellene was avoided as a leper. If a stevedore, he was cut off from communication with steamers. If a navvy, he was hindered from working. Imports from Greece, or consignments to Hellenes in Smyrna, Aivali, and elsewhere, could not be removed from the ships' holds. Customers were warned not to deal with Greek merchants and were left under no illusion as to the consequences of disobedience. Shops had to close and their owners to sell out their stock and goodwill for anything they could get for them, and emigrate. The creditors of the owners of these shops and firms, mostly Europeans, were involved in the losses inflicted on the Greek traders. Husbandmen were informed that they must discontinue their labours in the field, or else suffer the loss of something more precious than their crops. In a word, the Hellenic element of the Turkish Empire was put under a ban and forbidden to work for existence.

The economic effects of this organised persecution proved much further reaching than its authors had foreseen. Many business firms were dissolved; others became bankrupt. Vast consignments of goods from abroad had to be sent back. Large orders were countermanded. All credit ceased, and commerce was at a standstill. Several prosperous Hellenes, in order to save their substance, obtained French or Italian nationality, and others whose attempts to follow their example failed, left the country, went to Greece, and agitated in favour of war.

Parallel with this drastic action went an anti-Hellenic campaign in the Turkish press, of which the object was to encourage the movement by furnishing grounds for its continuance. And it is fair to say that these allegations were something more than flimsy pretexts. Turkish publicists pointed out that the end of the war was not the end of the hostility which had brought on the war. The causes were still operative. Ottoman Greeks, not satisfied with the spoils of the last campaign, looked with wistful eyes on the coast of Asia Minor, opposite to the annexed islands, and cherished the belief, as well as the hope, that that too would be incorporated with the kingdom of Greece. And this faith acted as an incentive to a propaganda which tended to sap the foundations of the empire. Ottoman Greeks, it was affirmed, emulating the example set them by Averroff, taxed themselves voluntarily for the purpose of enabling King Constantine's ministers to acquire new warships. Many of the young men went over to Greece to serve in the army or the navy there, as though they were citizens of the country and not the sultan's subjects. A large number of them had actually enlisted in the Greek Army and fought against the Turks during the war. Pursuant to a clause in the Peace Treaty, these offenders had to be included in the general amnesty, but they were known to their Moslem neighbours, who hated them intensely and deemed death a mild punishment for their perfidy. The government might pardon, but the people felt impelled to punish.

Utterances of this tenor stiffened with hard facts, which it was impossible to deny, accomplished their purpose. The Moslem population boiled with rage against the enemy within the gates. The boycott was envenomed with personal injuries and occasional acts of lawless violence. Thousands of the Greeks were ruined, their Moslem neighbours were impoverished, the state coffers were depleted, and the task of reorganisation seemed impossible.

Forcible Transportation of Whole Populations

Shiploads of Moslem emigrants arriving about this time in Constantinople from the newly acquired Greek province of Macedonia poured oil on the flames of popular passion. These people, rich and poor alike, had quitted the soil of their fathers, over which the Greek flag now fluttered, in order to settle among their own co-religionists. They were counted by scores of thousands. I travelled with some of them myself. It has been asserted that their emigration was voluntary, as was that of the Bosniaks, when Austria occupied Bosnia and Herzegovina over thirty years ago. Doubtless this was true in many cases, but it can hardly be accepted as an adequate explanation, accounting for all the facts without reserve. The entire Moslem population of Bosnia, it was argued, did not abandon the home of their ancestors when Austria took possession of the country. A large percentage stayed behind and flourishes there to this day. I was told by some of the emigrants that they were warned to leave, that they accordingly sold out their possessions in haste and under unfavourable conditions, receiving but a tithe of their value, and that in many cases the proceeds of these compulsory sales were seized on various pretexts by gendarmes on the way to the seashore, where they arrived without even the means of paying their passage to Stamboul. As I had no means of sifting these tales, I cannot lay them before the British public either as indisputable facts, or as pure inventions.

But those and more piteous stories were narrated by the refugees to their own people in Turkey and were received by these with implicit trust. Distributed among various villages on the coast of Asia Minor, the emigrants gave detailed accounts of their experience, which, true, false, or highly coloured, raised the anti-Greek feeling to boiling point. It was then that bands of marauders were formed, sometimes with a sprinkling of the newcomers but mostly without them, which moved stealthily from village to village along the coast, ordering the Greek inhabitants to vacate their dwellings and quit the country without delay, and more than once enforcing the order with atrocious deeds of violence.

On June 12, a procession of men, women, and children arrived in the town of Phocea, carrying bundles. They were fugitives from the village of Gherakeuy which had just been pillaged by a band of Turks. Seeing them, the inhabitants of Phocea were struck with wild fear, rushed into their houses, bolted and barred the doors, and waited in anguish for the apprehended catastrophe. But nothing happened. Still the panic had taken such a firm hold of the people that by noon next day about a thousand of them had embarked on fishing smacks that were in the roadstead and sailed over to the island of Mitylene, where I saw and spoke to many of them.

In Phocea, there chanced to be four Frenchmen at the time, men of courage and generosity, two of whom I met subsequently, and as soon as they discerned that the fears of the inhabitants were likely to be realised, they proceeded to occupy four different houses, hoisted the French tricolour, and asked the Kaimakam to protect them. This official, who is described as a quiet easy-going man with no initiative or energy, gave them each a gendarme to see that no harm befell them. Phocea, where he dwelt, was a flourishing little town at the foot of a hill by the seashore, inhabited only by Greeks. As soon as they had received the protection demanded, the four Frenchmen opened wide their doors, so that in case of need the baited townspeople might take refuge under the French flag and save as much of their movable possessions as could be accommodated.

About 6 pm on Saturday evening, June 13, they described a band of armed men moving stealthily towards the town. At midnight, the first rifle reports were heard, but they were only signals from a troop on one side of the town which were answered by the troop on the other side. Before sunrise, the work of pillaging the houses had begun, and at break of day, volley after volley was fired. One house was burning. From all sides, frenzied human beings were rushing about the shore looking for barques or boats to convey them from the scene of carnage. But there were none within hailing distance. One young woman with her infant was so paralysed with fear that she got drowned, together with the child, in water that was scarcely deeper than a foot and a half.

Before the day was over, two steamers came in sight and the Frenchmen, who had given asylum to over seven hundred persons, contrived to get about three thousand on board these vessels. The fugitives, in their mad haste to get away, upset the boats more than once and were rescued with difficulty, after which they were conveyed to the island of Mitylene, where I saw many of them. Old men and women of seventy were beaten to death, or shot, or stabbed. I myself saw some of the wounded. The houses were gutted, and the articles which were not removed were smashed. The spoils were transported on camels, and the bands disappeared. Between forty and fifty persons are said to have been killed in one town during those days of terror, and as many in another town.

On June 12, the inhabitants of Serakeuy, a Greek village situated between Menemen and Smyrna, who had had wind of the doings of the bandits, and had given asylum to a number of the fugitives from Gherakeuy, hid all the women and children and went in search of firearms for their defence. During the night, the crack of rifle fire was heard, and at about 3.30 am, bands of Turks from various places bore down on the village and surrounded it. The Metropolitan bishop[19]

---

[19] The Metropolitan enumerates Harmandali, Belladjik, Kisseekeuy, and many others.

affirms that the bands were headed by several gendarmes on foot and three on horseback. A battle was then begun, which went on until 8 am, when the villagers, having exhausted their supply of ammunition, after having killed a considerable number of their assailants, agreed to lay down their arms, to cede their possessions and quit the country on condition that their lives were spared. The bandits made the promise and then massacred them indiscriminately. The number killed varies according to the sources of the narratives, but it would appear to be between forty and fifty.

When these bands first appeared, the Vali, who resides in Smyrna, where I heard from his own lips his version of what occurred, was requested by the Kaimakam to dispatch some gendarmes for the protection of the villagers, as there were only ten in Phocea. Now the Vali himself had very few to dispose of, for in his province, there are but 2,500 gendarmes all told, or say ten to every thousand inhabitants. And as a considerable percentage of these is told off for special service, such as the protection of churches, consular officials, the konak, etc., there are hardly more than five to the thousand inhabitants. Under these circumstances, he could spare only ten men, and these he dispatched at once.

Talaat Bey's 'Quos Ego'

As soon as Talaat Bey, the minister of the interior, heard what was happening, he was alive to the imperative necessity of putting an end to these disorders at once. Instead of delegating this task to a subordinate, he started for the coast of Asia Minor and telegraphed peremptory orders that pending his arrival the emigration should be hindered and the population tranquillised. Reaching Smyrna, he took a special train to Menemen, accompanied by the Vali of Aidin, Rahmi Bey, one of the most prominent members of the Young Turkish party. From the station of Menemen to the town, the distance is about ten minutes' walk. At the station, the minister found the entire population clamouring to be allowed to leave the place. Talaat addressed them soothingly, assured them of his protection and exhorted them to return to their houses. They refused, alleging that armed men were lying in wait to pillage their dwellings and kill them. The minister then undertook to walk in front of them side by side with the Vali, so that if any shots were fired, he and his friend would be the first victims. Thereupon, they assented, and the procession set out. On the way, the Greeks pointed to a man in hiding and accused him of being one of the terrorist band. Talaat had him arrested. As he was armed, and admitted that he was one of the troop of pillagers, he was taken into custody. Another was then discovered, and another. Scores were thus captured and put in prison. The minister gave orders that they were to be taken before a court-martial, tried summarily, and punished condignly. And he has assured me that some sixty have been condemned to penal servitude, most of them for a term of five years.

Opposite the island of Chios is the peninsula of Chesme, which has been inhabited by a Hellenic population from time immemorial. Tidings of the raids and massacres of the armed bands were quickly carried thither by fugitives, whose thrilling narratives needed no admixture of fiction to impress those who heard them. The entire population was stricken with maddening fear and without a shot fired, an enemy in sight, or a word of warning, they gathered together the most precious of their movable possessions, put them on board steamers, fishing smacks, and boats, and sought safety in flight, leaving their lands, houses, and furniture to anyone who liked to take possession of them. In this case, no direct pressure of any kind was put upon the inhabitants.

The criminals guilty of the massacres at Phocea and Serekeuy escaped with their booty before any arrests could be affected. But it does not follow that they will all continue to elude the toils. A commission of inquiry has been created to ascertain who the ringleaders were and to get evidence of their guilt. Already some of the minor offenders have been captured and dealt with. As soon as the prime movers or the men who actually killed any of the villagers have been apprehended, they will have short shrift. The court-martial will deal with them summarily.

This interposition of Talaat Bey was timely and, in a sense, decisive. It put an end, for the time being, to organised raids on Christian villages and encouraged the belief that the Ottoman Government is resolved to tread the way of legality and to suppress the barbarous outbursts of popular fanaticism which characterised the reign of Abdul Hamid and survived his downfall for a time.

Now throughout all this work of extirpation by violence, there must have been some one guiding spirit conducting and coordinating the various raids along the coast and impressing the ringleaders with the idea that the Central Government was behind it and would see that they and their men went unpunished even for murder. Who was that factor? It was certainly neither the cabinet as a whole, nor any member of the cabinet. Possibly, it was some influential outsider, or it may have been one of the bandits inspired by the example of the boycotters and by the utterances of the Press. As soon as blood had been copiously shed, the government left nothing undone to remedy the evil so far as it was still remediable and to keep it from spreading. Talaat Bey spent some twenty-three days on the coast rushing about from place to place, issuing orders to officials, dismissing negligent subordinates, calming the population, seeing that criminals were punished, and adopting measures for the protection of the lives and property of the Christians. One of his first measures was to induce Enver Pasha, the war minister, to employ ten thousand soldiers in this work of pacification.

War Loomed in Sight

One result of this combined action of boycotters and bandits was international in its character. The coast of Asia Minor opposite the annexed islands was practically freed from the Hellenic element so obnoxious to the Turks. Indeed, along the entire coast there are now left only four towns and villages which are occupied by Christians, and of these, the two most important count about thirty thousand inhabitants each. In this way, one of the chief obstacles to a compromise between the two countries on the subject of the islands has been displaced. That the Ottoman Government is delighted at this deliverance is certain, but it would be unjust to infer that it actively encouraged the deplorable excesses which were instrumental in bringing it about. On the contrary, as soon as compulsory emigration began to be enforced by massacres, the minister of the interior used every means at his disposal and enlisted the services of his colleagues and in particular those of the war minister, to suppress violence, to punish those guilty of crime, and to hinder the recurrence of similar excesses in the future.

I travelled with the Greek Minister of the Interior, M. Repouli, to the annexed islands, where we visited the refugees. About eighteen thousand of them were distributed over the island of Chios – men, women, and children, some thousands in tents and huts, and the bulk of them in the fields under olive and fig trees, or by the roadside on the coast. We also called at Mitylene, where over forty thousand fugitives from the terror of the bands were temporarily domiciled, besides over twenty persons maimed and suffering, who were being treated in the hospitals. The people who were on the island of Chios were mostly from Chesme, where there had been no disorders, and nearly all of them desired to return to their homes and expressed the hope that the government of King Constantine would espouse their cause and reinstate them by military force. The refugees in Mitylene, on the contrary, refused to return at any price, so terrorised were they by the horrors they had witnessed and the anguish they had undergone. The Greek Government was paying each of the adults five pence a day and giving them half that sum for each child.

This forcible transportation of entire populations from two mutually hostile countries worked with powerful effect upon the public mind of both. Fierce bellicose currents set in which the respective governments appeared impotent to stem. By way of protest, the Ecumenical Patriarch of Constantinople, having taken the opinion of the Ecclesiastical Council, issued a decree closing all the Orthodox churches and schools in the empire[20]. The Athens Government dispatched a note to the Porte, demanding the reinstatement

---

[20] June 8.

of the expelled populations in their houses and farms, adding that it disclaimed responsibility for the consequences of neglect to suppress the persecution. The Porte replied by assuming that the object of the solicitude of the Greek ministers was their own subjects, for whose protection it would duly provide, and it then proceeded to lay stress on the immigration of 200,000 Musulmans who, it alleged, had sought asylum in Turkey from the persecution against them in the Greek provinces of Macedonia[21]. The tone of this note was conciliatory, and the oral explanations given by the Turkish Minister in Athens strengthened this favourable impression. On June 19, the Porte invited the embassies at Constantinople to send representatives to the scenes of the recent excesses, in order to see for themselves that efficacious measures had been adopted to remedy the evils complained of, which were not seriously denied. Dragomans were accordingly despatched by the ambassadors, and those men, having visited the various places, are now drawing up their reports, which I understand shed a glaring light upon the recent past and characterise the guaranteed future by a note of interrogation.

Meanwhile, popular passion in both countries was in full blast. From the surviving Hellenic towns and villages of Asia Minor reports continued to come that the boycott was waxing more intense than ever, that persecution had become more subtle but not less effective, and that isolated murders had succeeded wholesale massacres. It is certain that these reports rest on a groundwork of solid fact, for they have been amply borne out by independent testimony. The financial losses

---

[21] The number of Moslems who quitted Greek territory was hardly more than seventy thousand. The remainder were emigrants from Bulgaria, Servia, and Montenegro.

which the boycott inflicted on Smyrna alone are colossal, and they have not yet ceased. Loud voices were lifted up in advocacy of war. Preparations for a conflict were made in Athens and Stamboul with feverish haste and with a disregard for expense which was not without a humorous side. Turkey had a powerful battleship on the stocks in Great Britain. Greece was in treaty for the purchase of two from the United States, which she finally acquired. The Ottoman Minister of the Marine, Djemal Pasha, set out for Paris to place orders for the immediate delivery of thirty hydroplanes, fourteen torpedo destroyers, and four submarines. In Greece, the naval reserves were called up and had been retained until further orders. The Turks, in their eager haste, consented to take delivery of some of their vessels before they were absolutely finished, so that they might be ready to meet the adversary on more or less equal terms. And, at last, even responsible statesmen thought they could predict with tolerable accuracy, the date of the impending war.

The Dawn, or False Dawn, of Peace

It was at this conjuncture that I ventured to offer my services to bring about a compromise between the two states. From the island of Mitylene, I decided to pay a visit to Talaat Bey, who was at this moment in Asia Minor. I had informed him several days in advance of my intention, and as there were no steamers from Mitylene to Smyrna, owing to the claim still put forward by Turkey to this island, I decided to start in a special steamer flying the Greek flag. In Mitylene, however, it was feared that this would prove impracticable, seeing that no Greek ship had appeared in Turkish waters for several weeks, and that exception might be taken to the vessel conveying me. I soon set this right, however, by telegraphing to Talaat Bey, apprising him of the circumstances and requesting him to give orders to allow me to enter the harbour of Smyrna. This request was courteously complied with and every facility accorded me. I then had long conversations with the Vali of Smyrna, Rahmi Bey, a man of ancient Turkish family, efficient fortune, tested patriotism, and stainless character, whose view of current events, even when they touch himself painfully in his family relations, is tinged with an undercurrent of fatalism, at once characteristic and seductive. He, too, suffered poignantly in his affections by the atrocities that accompanied or followed the war, but the form in which he alluded to those painful episodes was epical in its simplicity and objectivity.

Talaat Bey, who is a man of intrepid temper, vigorous intellect, retentive memory, and large views, received my overtures in the spirit of a statesman who sets the welfare of his country above personal and party considerations and is ready to pursue that at any and every cost. On certain points, he was firm. Thus, he declared it impossible to reinstate in their homes the refugees who had already left the empire, but he added that he would put an effectual stop to further emigration, compulsory or even voluntary, and would take a series of other tranquillising measures, on which it would, at the present moment, be premature to dwell. He agreed, however, to appoint a mixed commission to assess the value of the immovable, and as far as feasible the movable, possessions of the refugees of both states and to strike a balance between them. He also acquiesced in my suggestion that in case the projected commission should be unable to agree, they would refer their divergent appreciations to the summary ruling of foreign arbiters. In a word, he spoke and behaved like a man gifted with a fine sense of the attainable in international politics and capable of schooling patriotic sentiments into fair-minded proposals and of discerning and appreciating the two sides of every question, however closely it might touch him. He approved himself as Turkey's real statesman, her one strong man. Gulliver, I fancy I hear the Greeks remark, was also a strong man, a giant compared with the Lilliputians, and yet the Lilliputians contrived to bind him.

Into an exposé of the practical consequences of these conversations, this is not the moment to enter. Sufficient to say that I soon felt justified in announcing, as I did, that the danger of war was, for the time being, eliminated, and the likelihood of a Greco-Turkish agreement had become considerable. What further developments the situation thus happily created may undergo in the near future, events, over which the Ottoman Government has apparently not complete control, will reveal. For the present, I have nothing more to say on the subject, except that the majority of the Greeks, including the Ecumenical Patriarchate, are pessimistic.

"If I Were King of Arcadia!"

Albania still continues to be a tangled skein which resists all attempts at unravelling. Not only does anarchy choke every enterprise, public and private but its aspects are so many and so baffling that they cannot all be connoted by any one name. In the South, the Epirotes are advancing steadily, capturing towns and villages, and threatening even Berat. Despite the exhortations of M. Venizelos and the orders of M. Zographos, they have occupied the city of Koritza, which was evacuated by the Albanian troops. In the centre, the insurgents still have the upper hand and are extending their sway. According to the most recent newspaper reports, which must be carefully sifted before being accepted, the important town of Berat has surrendered to the insurgents, who appeared before it provided with artillery. In the North, the Serbs and Montenegrins are hovering around the vague frontiers watching for a pretext to rush in. At Durazzo, in sight of the foreign warships, the monarch shares his mite of power with the cabinet, the Commission of Control, the officious Dutch officers, and the diplomatic representatives of Europe.

While all these political sections are waging war upon each other, the money advanced by the powers is being wasted – not through any fault of the finance minister but as a consequence of the situation – upon arms and ammunition which produce no effect upon the enemy. And all the sources of economic life are sealed up. The fields are neglected. Crops have not been reaped. There is hardly any internal trade and no foreign commerce to speak of, except in weapons of war. Poverty, which for ages has been a mark of the Albanian people, is now deepening into acute misery. Hunger has become a fruitful parent of disease. Hardly anywhere in the new state can an industrious workman find something to do and turn an honest penny by his toil. Sixty thousand people are said to be starving. By the time winter comes around, famine will be stalking the land.

The king, one reads, convoked a council, to which many notables outside the cabinet were admitted, including Ismail Kemal. The suggestions of these advisers touched every extreme of enterprise and forbearance. Some urged the necessity of imploring the powers to rescue the nation from its desperate plight. Others held that only the Commission of

Control can accomplish anything, and that the one thing now needful is to hand over all effective authority to that respectable body. And this view is said to be making headway in Europe. After all, it is urged, even the insurgents respect the Commissioners whom they look upon as the spokesmen of the powers. These delegates are men of experience. They have no interests of their own to further, no prejudices or leanings to blur their judgment, and can, therefore, address themselves to the work of regeneration wholeheartedly. To them, consequently, a task would be feasible which, to a cabinet, would be sheer impossible, seeing that all currents are set against every other institution.

Will an Albanian Heptarchy Solve the Problem?

I have seen the Commission of Control at work in various parts of Albania, and I have heard the results frankly and exhaustively discussed. It was pointed out without disparagement of the political discernment or resourcefulness of its members, that the insurgents of Shiak and Tirana negotiated amicably and often but made no headway. With the rebellious Epirotes, they also treated and concluded an agreement, but it proved a dead letter. With the peace-breakers of the North, they charged Colonel Phillips to deal, and he has dealt efficaciously. It was they who endeavoured to dissuade the king from keeping the Mirdites and Malissores at Durazzo. Yet it was the Mirdites and Malissores who, despite their great military defects, kept the insurgents from capturing that city and forcing the royal family to flee a second time. It was the Commission of Control, the critics add, which, when the Mirdites were already in Durazzo, about to enlist in the gendarmerie, besought the prince to dismiss them to their homes and warned him in express terms that his refusal to acquiesce in this advice would entail 'fatal consequences' to his rule. It is the Commission of Control, which, so far from being equal to the task of governing all Albania, has not been able to tackle some of the more pressing problems of Scutari and which left scores of urgent telegrams addressed to them on those subjects without any answer whatever. Those are some of the strictures which were passed on the commission by persons who can claim a hearing for their opinions.

Government by Commission is always a cumbersome, defective, and capricious mechanism, from which, even at its best, satisfactory results are not to be expected. And it is at its best when the members are all men acquainted with the country and the people, conversant with the momentous questions with which they have to deal, possessed of faith in the feasibility of their task, agreed upon a programme, provided with the means of carrying it out, and able to discourse with the public in the national idiom. Now, according to the critics of that institution, none of these conditions is fulfilled in the case of the present commissioners, all of whom are most honourable, well-meaning public servants but lack some of the qualities essential to success. Thus, they are often divided amongst themselves as to the wisdom of a measure to be taken; they are divided among themselves even on the question of the viability of the new state; with a single exception they do not speak or read the language of the country; they have no coherent programme, and if they had, they lack the means of realising it. But even if one could afford to overlook all these disabilities, there would still remain the decisive circumstance that a civil institution like the Commission of Control is not a suitable agency for fusing the discordant elements of the population into one political body and equipping this body with organs for self-preservation and constitutional growth. Only a clear-headed man of iron will and fearless temperament, resourceful, enterprising, and audacious, operating with an organised army at his back, and an adequate amount of money in the state coffers, and provided with a lease of dictatorial power for at least two or three years could hope to grapple with the task of building up a solid state out of the raw materials afforded by Albania. An organised army and sound finances are the two indispensable conditions of success.

Among the natives, who, in a matter which concerns them so closely, ought to be preferred to strangers, I find one man fully qualified, as I believe, to take in hand the financial and civil administration of the country. I have watched him at close quarters, studied his methods, analysed the results, and cannot but admire his sincere public spirit, the breadth of his views, his comprehensive knowledge of details, his marvellous capacity for work, and his winsome manner which has extorted even the esteem of political adversaries. He possesses at once the courage to say No to his best friends and the inestimable gift of being able to deprive a categorical refusal of its sting. That man is the present finance minister, M. Nogga. As commissioner of the powers, at the head of the entire civil administration of Albania, he would, I believe, ensure the fullest measure of positive results attainable under given circumstances.

On the subject of the military task, which in the present position of affairs is equally pressing, I am not entitled to demand a hearing, but I have discussed the matter with competent judges who are. In Scutari, I saw how Colonel Phillips addressed himself to what many of his colleagues deemed a desperate problem, and I was most favourably struck with his marvellous energy and resource, his knowledge of the workings of the native mind, and certain other qualities which have won for him the confidence and attachment of Moslems and Christians alike. But as any extension of this brilliant officer's powers is certain to be vetoed, it is needless to press his claims further.

Young Turkey Exclaims: "Barkis Is Willin"

In Stamboul, I have had many earnest conversations on this topic with my friend, Talaat Bey, with Izzet Pasha, and other prominent officials, military and civil. And as their utterances are likely to interest the general public I set them down here, as nearly as possible in the words of the principal speakers. "We Turks no longer harbour any designs on Albania. We have entered it as a dead loss in our political ledger, and wound up that part of our account for good. Politically, therefore, we are wholly disinterested, and any contribution we may offer to the solution of the puzzling Albanian problem is quite free from unavowed objects, and springs solely from the fellow-feeling we still cherish for our co-religionists who form a large majority of the population there."

"We recognise, as all Europe does, the necessity of creating a trained military force as the first step towards any kind of progress, or even consolidation. This can be accomplished only by a military man of experience in the field, who has a fair knowledge of the people, a man willing to devote himself to the task, and ready to depart when it is performed. Now, such a man is Izzet Pasha. His titles to respect and confidence are widely known and freely acknowledged. If he were entrusted with the mission under conditions enabling him to carry it out unhindered, our government would allow him to act as Europe's Commissioner and would send with him a sufficient number of Albanian officers who are now actively engaged in our army, to form the cadres of the Albanian forces. This free gift would facilitate Izzet's task considerably. He would not remain more than two or three years in the country and would withdraw at the end of that period, when the powers could hand over the organised army to any Prince they liked to appoint."

With Izzet Pasha himself, I also talked the matter over. This officer, who speaks German and French fluently, takes a very sensible view of the situation and is under no illusion as to the difficulties and dangers that will confront anyone who seeks to perform constructive work in Albania. "I am an Albanian myself," he said, "although neither my upbringing nor my later experience entitles me to make this claim. Still, I have been in the country, I am acquainted with many Albanians; I believe I understand their qualities and defects, and I can utilise both for the accomplishment of the task set. I am acquainted with Prenk Bib Doda, with Essad Pasha, and with other prominent Albanians. But I must have a free hand,

and be quite untrammelled. Unless this condition were guaranteed in advance I should decline the mission definitively, and every self-respecting organiser who means business and has his work at heart would do the same. As for money, I should like to say that while nothing can be accomplished without it, the amount which I deem necessary and adequate is very much less than the most moderate estimates made by Western Europeans who are unacquainted with Albania. I would undertake to do the work of forming a well-trained army capable of taking the field and effectively defending the frontiers at a cost which would astonish most Europeans by its relative insignificance. But as I stated already, while quite willing to accept the mission under the condition laid down from the powers of Europe, I do not feel in the least disposed to strive after it."

E. J. Dillon

The Contemporary Review, July–December 1915

One of the most instructive instances of this series of unedifying efforts to bribe and gull emanated from Count Julius Andrassy, who embodied his offer in an article lately published in Vienna[22]. That Hungarian statesman undertook on behalf of the Dual Monarchy, to forego all claims on Albania, to divide it up into sections, and to assign these as sops to the various interested states. One knows how greatly Austria took the Albanian problem to heart, and how resolved she was, come what might, to have it solved in her own way. How strong that resolve was may be inferred from the fact that more than once when that solution seemed unattainable, war loomed in sight. Thus, the withdrawal of the Montenegrins from Scutari was insistently urged under threat of war. The evacuation of Durazzo by the Serbs was demanded under the penalty of armed violence. And the reader may remember how imminent hostilities appeared during the heated and protracted discussions about Djakova, in which the writer of this article took a mediating part.

Well, "as Count Andrassy's article shows, the results of all those diplomatic exertions and one of the constant aims of

---

[22] In the Neue Freie Presse of Vienna, August, 1915.

Austria's policy were thrown to the winds, the moment it became desirable to win over Greece to the Central Empires. What had been vital to the Habsburgs a few months before had now become immaterial. "It was only in accord with Italy," wrote Count Andrassy, "that we could desire an independent Albania." But since Italy has occupied Valona, the best solution of the Albanian question from the Austro-Hungarian point of view would be the incorporation of the Southern portion of Albania in Greece, while the remainder would continue to form an autonomous state under the Greek dynasty." And on the strength of this generous concession, Count Andrassy exhorted Venizelos to gather his countrymen together in the camp of the two Central Empires and qualify for the prize.

But in vain was the net spread in the sight of the bird. Venizelos knows with whom he is dealing and can estimate aright the value of the promises extorted by necessity from each of the touters for Greece's co-operation. He it was who assented to the concessions which Serbia, solicited by the Entente, was prepared to make to Bulgaria as a peace offering and a pledge of friendship. In that, his object was the weal of all the Balkan States. And for a time, he really believed that Bulgaria would redeem her promise, accept the concessions, and resuscitate the Balkan League. The loss of that generous illusion was compensated by a deeper insight into human character – of the Balkan variety.

By the terms of the secret accord of Bucharest, Serbia was not free to make any retrocession of territory to Bulgaria without the assent of Greece. That assent being given, Serbia's generous offer was laid before the play-actors of Sofia, whose assumed susceptibilities to motives of honour and honesty filled the Entente Powers with hope. But Ferdinand and Radoslavoff proceeded to general mobilisation, and the Allies, it is fair to say, were greatly surprised. Venizelos then employed all his powers of argument and suasion to obtain King Constantine's authorisation to follow suit and summon the Greek Army to the colours.

E. J. Dillon

BEJTULLAH DESTANI (13.08.1960–)

British-Albanian scholar. Bejtullah Destani was born in Prizren in Kosovo and went to school there. He studied political science in Belgrade in the 1980s, where he published his first book, A Selektivna bibliografija knjiga o Albaniji, 1850–1984 (Selective Bibliography of Books about Albania, 1850–1984), Belgrade 1986. In 1991, in view of the increasingly perilous situation in his native Kosovo, he immigrated to London, where he has since lived. Destani has devoted himself to Albanian studies, in particular to research on British-Albanian cultural relations and has made many significant discoveries in British archives and libraries. He was appointed First Secretary of the new Embassy of Kosovo in London in October 2008 and was made Minister Counsellor at the Embassy in London and in September 2022) was appointed Embassy of Kosovo in Rome as Deputy Head of Mission.

In 1997, Bejtullah Destani founded the Centre for Albanian Studies in London initially very much a one-man show, and has managed, as head of this centre, to publish or republish a number of important works in Albanian studies.

1. Harry Hodgkinson: Scanderbeg, London 1999.

2. M. Edith Durham: Albania and the Albanians, Selected Articles and Letters, 1903–1944, Bejtullah Destani (ed.), 2001.

3. Dayrell R. Oakley-Hill: An Englishman in Albania, Memoirs of a British Officer, 1929–1955. London 2002.

4. Duncan Heaton-Armstrong: The Six Month Kingdom – Albania 1914, Bejtullah Destani (ed.), 2004.

5. Arthur Evans: Ancient Illyria, Bejtullah Destani (ed.), London 2007.

6. Edward Lear in Albania, Bejtullah Destani and Robert Elsie (ed.), 2008.

7. Albanian Greatest Friend – Aubrey Herbert and the Making of Modern Albania, preface by Noel Malcolm, Bejtullah Destani & Jason Tomes (ed.), London 2011.

8. Sir Arthur Evans: Albanian Letters: Nationalism, Independence and the Albanian League, Bejtullah Destani & Jason Tomes (ed.), The Centre for Albanian Studies, London 2017.

9. The Cham Albanians of Greece-A Documentary History, Bejtullah Destani & Robert Elsie (ed.), London 2012.

10. The Balkan Wars, British Consular Reports from Macedonia on the Final Years of the Ottoman Empire, Bejtullah Destani & Robert Elsie (ed.), London 2013.

11. Albanian Dialects, Prince Louis-Lucien Bonaparte, Bejtullah Destani (ed.).

12. M. Edith Durham: The Blaze in the Balkans, Selected Writings 1903–1941, Bejtullah Destani & Robert Elsie (ed.), London 2014.

13. Nicholas Bethell, The Albanian Operation of the CIA & MI6, 1949–1953, Robert Elsie & Bejtullah Destani (ed.), 2015.152.

14. Kosovo, A Documentary History: From the Balkan Wars to World War II edited by Robert Elsie & Bejtullah Destani, 2018.

15. MINORITIES IN THE MIDDLE EAST: Christian Minorities 1838–1967 10 volumes, 6500 pages; Editor: B. Destani.

16. MINORITIES IN THE MIDDLE EAST: Druze Communities 1840–1974 4 volumes, 2000 pages; Editor: B. Destani.

17. MINORITIES IN THE MIDDLE EAST: Kurdish Communities 1918–1974 4 volumes, 2000 pages; Editor: B. Destani.

18. MINORITIES IN THE MIDDLE EAST: Muslim Minorities in Arab Countries 1843–1973 4 volumes, 2400 pages; Editor: B. Destani.

19. MINORITIES IN THE MIDDLE EAST: Religious Communities in Jerusalem 1843–1974 4 volumes, 2090 pages; Editor: B. Destani.

20. The Zionist Movement and the Foundation of Israel 1839–1972 10 volumes, 8000 pages; Editor: B. Destani.

21. Albania and Kosovo: Political and Ethnic Boundaries 1867–1946 1 volume, 1100 pages; Editor: B. Destani.

22. Ethnic Minorities in the Balkan States 1860–1971 6 volumes, 4400 pages; Editor: B. Destani.

23. Montenegro: Political and Ethnic Boundaries 1840–1920 2 volumes, 1800 pages; Editor: B. Destani, with an introduction by former President M. Djukanovic.